COGNITIVE DEVELOPMENT AMONG SIOUX CHILDREN

GILBERT VOYAT

*City College and the Graduate Center
of the City University of New York
New York, New York*

in collaboration with

STEPHEN R. SILK

*University of California at San Diego
School of Medicine
La Jolla, California*

and

GAYLA TWISS

*Indian Health Service
Pine Ridge, South Dakota*

PLENUM PRESS • NEW YORK AND LONDON

Library of Congress Cataloging in Publication Data

Voyat, Gilbert.
    Cognitive development among Sioux children.

    (Cognition and language)
    Bibliography: p.
    Includes index.
    1. Oglala Indians—Psychology. 2. Indians of North America—South Dakota—Psy-
chology. 3. Cognition and culture. 4. Piaget, Jean, 1896–   . I. Silk, Stephen R. II. Twiss,
Gayla. III. Title. IV. Series.
E99.O3V68 1983   155.4′13′08997   83-2463
ISBN 0-306-41276-4

©1983 Plenum Press, New York
A Division of Plenum Publishing Corporation
233 Spring Street, New York, N.Y. 10013

Printed in the United States of America

To my wife Mary,
with all my love and gratitude

G. V.

Acknowledgments

Primarily our thanks and deep gratitude go to the Indian community on the Pine Ridge Reservation, without whose help, involvement and commitment this study would not have been possible. So many people in the community have in one way or another contributed to this work that it would require almost another book to cite them all.

Specifically, however, we would like to thank those of the staff of the Mental Health Program whose help has been invaluable:

Mr. M. Roscow, Acting Director of the Program, Mr. H. Zephier, Director of the hospital, Miss E. Gill, Dr. E. Maynard, Mr. R. Church, Mr. D. Ostendorf, Mrs. G. Twiss, Mrs. F. Afraid of Hawk, Mr. H. Bear Runner, Mrs. D. Waters, Miss. Y. Giago, Mrs. L. Cuny, Mrs. P. Black Elk, Mrs. L. Gipp, J. Bachant, Mrs. H. Vessley, Mrs. D. McLaughlin.

Among the many in Oglala to whom we are indebted we would like to thank:

Mr. L. Gross, School Principal and Mr. E. High White Man who drove us to the parents of many of the children and made us accepted in many families.

In Manderson our thanks go to Mr. D. Wince, Mrs. Cash, Mrs. H. Twiss, Mrs. C. Twiss, and Mrs. S. Buffington.

Our deep gratitude goes to the staff and the members of the Headstart Program in particular Mr. L. Bear Heals, and to the staff and the members of the Parent Child Center (PCC) in particular Mr. T. Allen.

We would like to thank all those who have contributed to give us their pedagogical and educational suggestions: Mr. B. Lay, Mr. R. Cournoyer, Mr. R. Pentilla, Mr. D. Kundson, Father Welshon, Mr. L. Vocu, Father Labaj, Mrs. A. Ross.

We would like to thank all the parents and the children themselves for their indispensable role in this research.

Finally in order not to make this kind of reading unduly distracting we have used he instead of he and/or she and ask for the reader's indulgence.

Contents

History of an Act of Faith

Gilbert Voyat, Ph.D.

Professor of Psychology
The City College and The Graduate Center
City University of New York

INTRODUCTION

This study is cross-cultural, cognitive, and social-psychological in character. More importantly, it is a study of people, of children – and specifically of Sioux children. It is my hope that it may in some measure counter the fact that Native Americans are widely misunderstood, despite, or more likely because of, the "fame" bestowed upon them by movies and television.

Diamond [1] has pointed out that "acculturation has always been a matter of conquest. Either civilization directly shatters a primitive culture which happens to stand in its historical right of way or a primitive social economy, in the grip of a civilized market, becomes so attenuated and weakened that it can no longer contain the traditional culture." There have been two phases in the white man's conquest of the North American Indians. The first of these was conquest by force. "In 1876," writes Steiner [2], "George Armstrong Custer surprised a wintering camp on the Little Big Horn River but was 'wiped out.' He was killed on the first assault in the middle of the Little Big Horn River. It was published that each Indian killed cost the government one million dollars. The Indian population was down to forty-four thousand souls." The economic factor had already played a crucial role, of course, in the conflict between pioneers and Indians; the lust for gold, silver, and land must be considered the chief motivational force in the systematic destruction of the Native Americans by the white man's advancing civilization. The banner of Christian morality held aloft by the institutionalized religion of the Europeans put few checks on the killing of Indians. In this first phase of conquest, genocide constituted part of the

"American know-how" of the settlers; for the Indians, it was part and parcel of the acculturation process.

The second phase of conquest is still under way. For the most part it no longer involves naked force. This new type of domination makes technology its means, acculturation its end, and places history in the upside-down perspective so familiar from the world of the "western."

So strong is this stereotype that on my first visit to South Dakota, out riding, I half-expected Indian braves to appear on the hilltops and charge down to attack us. Such things no longer happen, of course, but, as I shall try to show, the war between white man and Indian has changed only its form, not its content.

Richard T. Little, chairman of the Oglala Sioux Land Committee, leader of the Sheep Mountain project and member of the Tribal Council, once concluded a letter to then President Nixon in the following terms: "You say I am a silent, stoic, and peaceloving member of the first Americans. Remember this: I have also fought your wars. I planted the stars and stripes on Iwo Jima. I have been your excuse for your economic disasters. I have made your heroes of the past century, and I am the guy who loses the battles on your television shows and makes your children laugh..."[3] Richard Little is a Sioux. He wears a headband and long hair. He does not offer a friendly welcome to whites whether they hate Indians or love them. He uses the word "we" much more often that the word "I," for he does not speak for himself alone. He knows himself; he also knows that he is a symbol. He carries in himself a deep sense of history, and he truly represents his people because his people define him. He is traditional and proud, he does not compromise and he is not easily fooled. He does not stand for himself alone but for his people as a whole.

The reader will have to forgive me if my tone in what follows seems too personal for an introduction to a "scientific-cognitive" study. Such introductions usually contain a specific explanation about methodology, and supply the background that will supposedly enable the student to make his way less painfully through percentages, comparisons, and detailed analyses of results. Approached in this way, a cognitive study of Indian children might well be expected to remain dry and overladen with experimental data. This has not been my intention, however. Rather, in view of the topsy-turvy perspective through which Native American history and culture is generally viewed by whites, I sought to turn my own professional perspective upside down. One of the problems of psychology is its cult of specialization. Studies of cognitive development, in particular, rarely incorporate an epistemological and global point of view, for they are prey, like the discipline as a whole, to the technological ideology which identifies specialization with precision.

When I first decided to spend several months in Porcupine, South Dakota, at an Indian reservation, most of my New York friends and colleagues wondered what I would or could do, lost in such an "unfriendly" part of the country. At the time I did not quite know how to justify it myself. So I talked vaguely of the urgent necessity for cross-cultural studies, even though I was well aware how much had already been published by anthropologists, psychologists, and cultural psychoanalysts. After all, Erikson had long ago written Childhood and Society, and Vine Deloria was now urging that the Indians be left alone....

So strong was my conviction that a relevant study was possible, however, that I persisted. At the same time I made some firm resolutions before starting out. The first was that I would somehow make the research and its findings serve the people who were the subject of them. I promised myself I would talk to the parents about the significance of my Piagetian experiments to them. This, I knew, would call for adaptation on my part: I would have to get off the pedestal of professional jargon and endeavor to undergo an "acculturation process" of my own vis-a-vis the Sioux. A second resolution had to do with the nature of the experimentation itself. Although I was setting out to collect results for my own comparative purposes, I felt sure that my findings could have an application, via teachers or community leaders, among the Sioux themselves, and my research was designed with this in mind.

My success in this area is still hard to gauge. But I did abide by my resolutions, even though there were times, I must confess, when I almost regretted having made them. It is much easier to work as a "pure observer" than to share results and by so doing become an active participant in a community that has no a priori reason to trust you.

First arrival at Pine Ridge Indian Reservation gave me a real sense of what it is to be a foreigner. This experience was both similar and different to the culture shock I had suffered when I first came to the United States as a Swiss with no English. At that time my language difficulties had characteristically given rise to a depression, despite the sympathy and forebearance shown me by my colleagues in Project MAC at MIT's Electrical Engineering Department, where I was doing research on artificial intelligence. My adaptation to "mainstream American culture" proceeded very slowly, and in many ways the process is still unfinished. It involved much more than linguistic factors, of course. Superficially, Boston was simply a bigger - much bigger - version of the village I had left in Switzerland. But there were two things which very soon struck me. The first was people's truly amazing friendliness. They were full of understanding about my difficulties of adaptation. They helped me constantly. They empathized with my concerns. I made many friends in a very short time. The real problem was not making friends, how-

ever, but how superficial these friendships were. This was in strong
contrast to European customs. In Switzerland it takes months to make
friends; in the United States it seemed to take about a day. As
Diamond has written [4], "In machine-based societies, the machine has
incorporated the demands of the civil power or of the market, and the
whole life of society, of all classes and grades, must adjust to its
rhythms." It is true that one of the properties of a capitalist
civilization is its mobility, its rhythm, sometimes positively described as pragmatic flexibility; but it is equally true that one of
the sociological consequences of such a system is the uncertainty and
superficiality of human relationships.

The second fact which struck me was that most conversation in
the United States had as a metatheme competition and money. Not that
the Swiss did not discuss these matters. On the contrary. But they
did not discuss them to the exclusion of all else, whereas in Boston
or New York they sometimes seemed to supply the subtext of all communication. Europe, it seemed to me, had not yet reached this state
of affairs.

Now, two years later, speaking English albeit with a heavy
French accent, I arrived at Pine Ridge and found myself, paradoxically, "back home." This was not a matter of language. The Sioux
have two languages: English, which I now understood, and Lakota,
which I still do not understand except for the traditional "waste,"
which means "good" and should not be used too frequently. (As it was
my entire vocabulary, however, I could hardly avoid overusing it.)
Nor was it a matter of landscape: Switzerland is covered with mountains while South Dakota has none to speak of. No, it was a matter
of how people were. Ironically, after two years of easy but facile
friendships, I found myself among people who acted quite differently.
Indians looked at me and smiled. They were superficially cooper-
ative. Children were eager to please and give the right answer to my
questions. Parents would say "yes" all the time in order to get rid
of me as quickly as possible. And I had the feeling of not really
communicating at all. The Indians did not empathize with me, did not
help me, did not share my concerns, and, needless to say, remained
unconvinced as to the urgent necessity of cross-cultural studies.
Yet I felt at home, because I knew that this reception was very much
like the one that a foreigner might encounter in my own village in
Switzerland. Lerner [5] has remarked that "The Frenchman guards his
individuality by maintaining le soi (his own self) inviolate from the
impingements of the public arena." These Indians were doing the same
thing.

It took many months, but, finally, I made friends. Not superficial friends: real friends.

There, however, the similarity ends. When I began to talk with
my new friends, the content of their conversation turned out to re-
semble nothing I had ever before encountered. So far from making

competition, money, status, or material comfort the metathemes of
their exchanges, the Sioux explained everything by reference to God,
Earth, animals and plants. Their essential realities lay in their
symbols. To quote Diamond again [6], "History to them is the recital
of sacred meanings within a cyclic, as opposed to a lineal, perception of time. The merely pragmatic event, uninvolved with the sacred
cycle, falls, as it were, outside history, because it is of no importance in maintaining or revitalizing the traditional forms of
society." The ever-present sense of the sacred, the idea of being in
harmony with the earth, and the overarching concept of reciprocity
were as alien to my Swiss background as they were to the white North
American culture. At the same time, it would be quite possible to
stay in the Pine Ridge Indian Reservation without ever becoming aware
of these underlying cultural themes. In face of such complex and
occult principles, I found myself at once daunted and seduced by the
enormous potential power of this people. In this frame of mind I
thought often of an Indian tale told by Jaime De Angulo [7]:

> ...Then Bear called: "Good Night, Mountains, you must
> protect us tonight. We are strangers but we are good
> people. We don't mean harm to anybody. Good night Mister
> Pine Tree. We are camping under you. You must protect us
> tonight. Good night Mister Owl. I guess this is your home
> where we are camped. We are good people, we are not look-
> ing for trouble, we are just traveling. Good night, Chief
> Rattlesnake. Good night everyone. Good night, Grass
> People, we have spread our bed right on top of you. Good
> night, Ground, we are lying right on your face. You must
> take care of us, we want to live a long time..."
> Fox said, "Oh, look! The sun is coming back on the other
> side!"
> "No, little boy, that's the moon. He is the elder brother
> of the sun and he works at night."
> "Oooh! Well, good morning, Mister Moon."
> "No, silly, you mean good night."
> "No, I don't. It's good morning for the moon."
> "All right. Go to sleep."
> Bear was already snoring. And now Antelope sat up. She
> looked into the shadows and sang softly a song to the
> night. It said: "Dream for my child so that he will have
> power."

Back in New York, the ethnocentricity of white America was borne
in upon me once more. I spent a good deal of time explaining to
otherwise educated people that the American Indians I had gotten to
know did not usually eat buffalo or live in teepees. So far as the
outward trappings of everyday life are concerned, Indian culture
seems all but totally assimilated. Yet this culture does have a
specificity, one having to do not with overt behavior but with inner
being, with a "religious" apprehension of reality.

So much, at least, I learned on my first visit to Pine Ridge. Since then I have never had any difficulty justifying my field trips. But, of course, many more hurdles lay ahead in my attempt to understand what makes a Sioux a Sioux. My first reception at the Reservation had been so politely distant that I had come to feel the horses were almost more welcoming than the people. By the time I arrived at Pine Ridge for my second visit, the horses had lost a good deal of their interest.

It turned out that Gerald One Feather, an acquaintance of mine, was the new tribal leader. At first glance there is nothing spectacular about Gerald One Feather. He drives a pickup. He is married, with four children, to a Navajo. He lives near Oglala. He had a telephone, electricity, but no running water. He wears a stetson and sunglasses. As is true of all tribal leaders, forebears of his are said to have been among the signers of the treaty with the U.S. government. He talks slowly in a deep voice, with the help of images that would never come naturally to a white man's lips. He radiates moral authority, although, as he is at pains to explain, his position does not ipso facto give him any power. The authority he enjoys is perpetual, and essentially unaffected by the office he holds: it will endure even if he is not re-elected as tribal leader.

One day I was standing talking to Gerald in front of the Tribal Office in Pine Ridge when an old Indian came up to him and the two started talking Lakota. The old man kept pointing insistently at me, so when he went off I asked Gerald if their conversation had concerned me. "Yes," was Gerald's reply. "He was saying that you should not be here. Your place is elsewhere." And he left it at that.

Some time later, Gerald asked me what I was doing the next day, a Sunday. "Nothing in particular," I replied, upon which he announced that he would pick me up in the morning, and left without further explanation. Sure enough, the following morning Gerald drove over for me, along with his wife, children, and another Indian, Gerald Clifford. There was barely room for me in the car. Though quite mystified, I surmised that I was going to be taken on a sightseeing outing in the surrounding country. Gerald had quite another idea in mind, but I think he was still leaving his options open.

The fact is that Gerald much resembled the Mayan villager Eustaquio Ceme, whom Redfield [8] has described as "a very thoughtful man in that he considered persistingly and penetratingly many questions: religious, moral and political. He would pause when a problem occurred to him and take it away to give it thought; later he would set out in careful words the opinions or explanations or conceptions to which his cogitations had brought him. But he was primarily a man of action; he was a leader of his people in a period of transition and crisis."

Gerald drove to the nearby Rosebud Reservation. No sooner had the car stopped than his wife and children disappeared and I was led into the middle of a large gathering. This turned out to be a meeting of the American Indian Leadership Council. Gerald introduced me to the assembled company, explaining that I was studying the cognitive development of Indian children, and that I was very eager to talk about my results and their pedagogical implications. In reality I was very much less than eager at that moment to discuss anything, but of course I had no choice. So I took my courage in both hands and did my best. Question time brought queries not only about my professional activities at Pine Ridge but also about my childhood and private life. Naturally enough, my audience wanted an idea whom they were dealing with just as much as an account of my research. By the time the session ended I was exhausted. I must have managed to perform adequately, however, for this occasion inaugurated a new level of reciprocity between the Indians and me. In the immediate moment, I was only too thankful to withdraw from the spotlight into a corner and read the bylaws of the Council which someone had handed me.[9] In the preamble I read: "We members of the AILC bound by our Indian Heritage and aware of the obligations of that heritage to give of ourselves, unite in a determined effort to bring about the revitalization of the Indian People. By our united effort we will seek to attain our true identity as Indians, and thus recover the deep spiritual and human values of the Indian way and devote ourselves to reestablishing the living circle of Indian Society." Footnotes defined the use of the terms "spiritual" and "living circle": "By spiritual values it meant the submission to God, the Great Spirit, in an attitude of humility and prayer with the realization that power comes to man and all creation from God. There is no intent in AILC to create a new Indian Religion or to revive the old as it was. Rather we hope to recover the values that made the Indian's whole life a life lived in awareness and consideration of God. These religious values, we believe, will help the contemporary Christian Indian become the most authentic Christian of the denomination of his choice as well as the non-Christian to authentically commit himself to man and God." "By 'living circle of Indian society' is meant the bond of unity which circling through the Indian People makes them one. The circle or hoop as a symbol of unity is descriptive of a nation, a people united. When the circle is broken there is no more a nation, a people who are one. Rather there remains an assortment of individuals, each going his own way, opposing one another in envy and jealousy, all that is opposed to love and authentic kinship."

My chief concern now was how to apply Piagetian theory to Indian children whose symbolic thinking was so extensive. Before I could even begin to evaluate their grasp of conservation, space, time, or logical thought, however, I had to win the children's confidence. This was not a simple matter, and had it not been for Gayla Twiss, a Sioux woman, I do not believe I would ever have managed it.

For a long time I remained very pessimistic about the feasibility of getting the sort of cooperation I needed from the children, especially the very young ones. One hot day in Oglala, I was trying for the umpteenth time to get five four-year-olds involved, with so little success that I was even beginning to blame the kids themselves. How come they simply did not want to play, draw, and talk with me? I had tried smiling, laughing, talking in a soft voice, offering rewards - all to no avail. A kid would pick up a pencil for two seconds and set it aside. Or stare uncomprehendingly at me without saying a word. I was ready to pack up and go home, when Gayla solved the problem. She suggested we let the children play together by themselves first, then only very slowly intervene, working from the periphery of their activity, as it were, towards the center.

Gayla's approach worked perfectly, and I began to think she was more of a psychologist than I was. Her attitude, moreover, perfectly embodied Kurt Goldstein's principle that one "should never consider phenomena isolatedly and never compare phenomena observed in isolation. What we observe is embedded in the activity of the whole organism"[10].

Thanks to Gayla, then, as well as to Steve Silk and to many other Indian friends, I managed to open up the needed avenues of communication with the children of Pine Ridge. My despairing mood quickly changed into euphoria. Before long I developed a most unrealistic view of the "superiority" of the Indian kids we were studying. Once again, it took an Indian to straighten things out for me, and to make me realize that my exaggerated enthusiasm was a form of reverse discrimination. The Indian in question was Bob Morrison, Chief Holy Dance.

I first met Bob Morrison as we both watched the first moon landing on television, and on that occasion too he taught me a lesson. I made some trite remark about the moon landing being a great human achievement, and a vindication, for once, of technological progress. Bob kept silent for a minute or two, then replied: "We Indians used to worship the moon a long, long time ago. We always have done. Now the white man has got in too. We always had it."

As for my tendency to idealize the capacities of the Indian children, my chastening exchange with Bob in that connection went as follows.

"I think it's amazing that Indian children are able to hunt buffalo at the age of six," I said.
"You come from Switzerland, don't you?" asked Bob.
"Yes."
"There are mountains over there, right? And a lot of snow? How old were you when you learned to ski?"
"About six."

"Look," said Bob, "learning to ski is no easier than learning to hunt buffalo. Both things need good eyes, good hands, good legs, and all of them working well together. In Switzerland you have mountains and no buffalo. Over here we have buffalo but no mountains. That's where the whole difference is."

From then on I stopped being indulgent if an Indian cheated me. I started liking some Indians and disliking others. In short, the Indians at Pine Ridge had finally become ordinary people for me, just like those at home in my native Swiss village.

I have written here not about methodology, nor even about the experiments themselves whose results are presented in the main body of this book. Instead, I have written of my own feelings, of anecdotal events, of horses, and of my Indian friends at Pine Ridge. I have even tried to portray my subjective state while on the Reservation by quoting from an old Indian tale. My sole purposes in taking this tack has been to try to convey the fact that, though I went to South Dakota in order to develop a profile of the cognitive development of Indian children, that is not all that I was doing there. I have sought in the foregoing remarks to give some idea of the "real-life perspective" to which all the empirical data set forth in the following pages should be subordinated. If I have been all successful, I venture to hope that readers of this study will gain an insight into that reality far more quickly than was possible for me.

REFERENCES

1. S. Diamond, "Primitive Views of the World," Columbia University Press, New York, p. vi (1964).
2. S. Steiner, "The New Indians," Harper and Row, New York, p.321 (1968).
3. R. T. Little, Second Letter to President Nixon, In: "The Oglala War City," Pine Ridge, South Dakota, Vol. I, No. 4, July (1970).
4. Diamond, op. cit., p. viii.
5. D. Lerner, An American Researcher in Paris, In: "Studying Personality Cross-Culturally," Harper and Row, p. 434.
6. Diamond, op. cit., p. i.
7. J. De Angulo, "Indian Tales," Hill and Wang, New York, p. 13 (1953).
8. R. Redfield and A. Villa, "Chan Kom, a Maya Village," Carnegie Institution of Washington, Washington, D.C. Publication No. 448, (1934).
9. American Indian Leadership Council's bylaws, Rosebud (South Dakota) (1970).
10. K. Goldstein, Concerning the Concept of 'Primitivity,' In: "Primitive Views of the World," ed. S. Diamond, Columbia University Press, New York, p. 3 (1964).

Part I

I

General Introduction

Some controversies in psychology are not really controversies. For example, an almost eternal source of conflict amongst people of many fields has grown over the problem of how we think and learn. Can learning be described and analyzed solely by looking to factors outside the individual learner, do we do better to emphasize and describe hypothesized internal mechanisms of adaptation, or both? Shall we talk of native endowment, environmental influences or some combination of the two, when we seek to understand how we think? Do we do best to examine children or adults, conduct experimentation or scratch our collective chins, to analyze the development of knowledge? How to proceed?

If we step back for a moment and recall the way in which concern with matters of intelligence and thought have grown, we may see why much confusion remains. One of the major routes through which attempted understanding of cognition has passed, has been intelligence testing. Since a review of the literature would only add to the confusion already implicit and sometimes explicit in all IQ tests, we will not attempt one here. There are however, a few critical points which one could make. Intelligence testing grew as a primarily practical approach to making decisions of placement about people. When Binet [1], some 85 years ago, was given the task of devising a scheme for identifying mental defectives, he was not asked to offer an elaborate or even simple understanding of thought processes, or to focus on a qualitative description of the difficulty of defectives, but was rather directed towards finding an empirical tool with which one might make decisions of selection. Thus, although he and his many successors have, to varying degrees of significance, devised such measures, these IQ tests tend to leave us dry if our thirst is for an understanding of the way in which thought proceeds and grows. Thus, we may catalogue and sort, but these tests tell us little of all about the deep processes or mechanisms of thinking that lie beneath the manifest behavior that we empirically measure. We thus, may at times, make the quantitative analyses that a standard IQ test allows, but we should more often ask what then we have really understood.

A further point which we only introduce here and will expand upon later relates to the cultural relativity of an IQ test result. If it is true that such tests are empirically keyed, then one might very well ask if the scales drawn up in one cultural setting really represents a set of fair tasks in a diverse cultural setting. Thus, if in one setting correct response to a particular question seems to correlate highly with age and school performance and we then keep it as a good item on our IQ test, is it necessarily true that the same question will serve an identical function in a different cultural setting? Much evidence already suggests the cultural biases of IQ tests and this will be touched on again later. Let it be pointed out though, that when we seek to understand thinking and the growth of knowledge, there are these critical handicaps inherent in IQ testing with which one must reckon.

We then have two main points. For sure, Wechsler [2], when forming the WISC drew up his standardization sample with respect to factors such as geographic area, urban-rural residence, father's occupation, subject's sex, age, etc. However, even if we overlook the fact that mostly White children were sampled, we are still frankly left with the problem that after the test has been given we really don't know what has been measured.

Fortunately there are other ways in which we may address our-selves to the problem of knowing more about knowledge, learning, and thought, and we will seek to describe in considerable detail, one such approach to this task and a research project that has been car-ried out, embracing this approach, on the Pine Ridge Reservation in South Dakota with a population of Oglala Sioux Indians.

THE PINE RIDGE DEVELOPMENTAL STUDY

Introduction

Implicit in what we have said so far, is that the standard measures of intelligence, because of their very nature, give only a static measure which seeks to relate one individual's quantitative performance to another's. This is so because these tests assume that one's ability to think, his intelligence, may be estimated if we measure essentially the amount of knowledge that he possesses. A fundamentally different approach to understanding one's capacity to think has come from the years of careful thought and significant re-search done by the Swiss psychologist, Jean Piaget. His efforts have been largely devoted to uncovering the fundamental processes which underlie our capacity to reason. Thus, his efforts have been aimed more at elucidating the very processes which are available to us and allow us to gain knowledge, than in quantifying the contextual knowledge that we have gained.

Thus, the methodology of the research we shall describe contrasts very much with the standard testing approach, because it is essentially exploratory rather than static, and allows us the essential flexibility demanded by work with different ethnic groups, personalities, or social environments. We have undertaken a developmental study which seeks not to explore personality as a whole but rather the cognitive aspect of development, and in which we employ the Clinical Exploratory Method of Piaget. Thus, we shall focus mainly upon cognitive development and attempt to describe it in its normal socio-economic and ethnic environment.

Practical Implications

In Piaget's theory the child is actively involved in organizing his world of thought as he develops, and to understand this growing organization we must return to the child and examine the course of his thought through growth. He develops, for himself, his own cognitive structures and since this process of development is not only external, but goes on internally as well, it seems reasonable to assume that logic viewed from this end is not biased as much by the cultural context in which it is examined. Perhaps some examples, at this point, could better express the idea.

Our system of counting has as its base the number ten. The very word "decimal" and the use of the decimal point suggests the central role of "tens" as we count. One could devise a counting system with a different base, say base 12, for example. Our system of telling time has 12 as its base and thus, when we read a clock and we add 2 hours to 11:00 we get 1:00. We see then that 11 plus 2 equal 1. Any such counting system could be devised, and it just so happens that the ancient Mayas had a numerical system with a base of 20 for calculations, instead of base 10, as we have. Most importantly though, the logic of the internal relations in all of these systems is precisely the same among Mayas, among White, and among the clock watchers of the world. The logic of adding, subtracting and of other operations remains the same. Here is the important point. If we were to understand a concept like number, should we choose the system of the Mayas, the system of the clocks, or some other arbitrary system determined by cultural preference, or should we seek to evaluate such notions by examining the basic logical properties by which they are underlain? It seems safe to assume that if we seek to evaluate the development of the concept of number we must employ experiments dealing directly with number constructions. If we expect our measures to be culturally fair we must construct them not on the level of their cultural embodiment, but on a level of their logical properties.

Furthermore, one could note how remarkable it is that the Mayas discovered the number zero almost 1,000 years before it was discovered on the other side of the world, probably by the Arabs.

Two worlds, so far apart, understood the logical necessity of the use of zero to build the structure of numbers. We see here not a cultural necessity but the necessity of a given group to deal with its logic. We shall see that Piaget's experiments do deal with these basic logical processes, and not the essentially cultural attributes of thought.

The Mayas were also famous for the huge pyramids they built, on the top of which they placed their temples. Some of these pyramids were close to 300 feet high. Here too we should note that the cognitive apprehension of space and the way to organize objects in space was a logical necessity, for the construction of such pyramids, and geometric relations had, on some level, to be dealt with. Again, Piaget's views in his experiments are basic, since they deal with the very development of spatial organization.

Today, to see an Indian put up a tepee so that a sudden storm or blizzard will not move it, implies that he has a good grasp of spatial organization. It is the conic structure which confers stability, and this implies an empirical knowledge of principles of surface distribution and three dimensional geometry. Thus, if the Mayas of long ago, or contemporary Indian, White man, or anyone, can build stabile buildings, can count, can trade, and can share, we may infer the existence of basic logical invariances which are a product of the types of logical relations that are necessarily established between objects. This is one of the main aspects of a structural focus of the development of cognition, rather than a simple behavioral one, and is the basic point which underlies our work.

To further illustrate the notion of an underlying structure in cognition, we could point to a current controversy centering on Piaget's theory. Among many Berlyne [3], a behaviorist, has attempted to reduce Piaget's theory to a behaviorist one, and in so doing has completely misunderstood the essential organizing and re-structuring abilities of the individual. As an example of such an underlying structure we may cite the operation of transitivity. As a general principle, transitivity refers to the capacity to coordinate various positions in space or time into a unique trajectory. As it is manifested on a sensori-motor level in the very young child, it describes his ability to understand how an object behaves as it passes from position A, to position B, to position C; etc. that is to say it describes his ability to understand that the object follows a unique

path in its displacement. From the Piagetian point of view, as the
object follows path A B C, it is the arrows - the process of understanding - that is the critical focus. The Behaviorists would have it
that we examine the environment at point A, point B, Point C, and
from this deduce what principle might account for the subject's reaction. The basic difference here is that if we really do understand
the underlying process, the particular situation in which the operation occurs is irrelevant. Another way to say this is that once we
examine thought on the level of its underlying principles, factors
such as culture seem not to contaminate our results. Conversely, if
we do as the Behaviorists suggest, we cannot divorce ourselves from
the specific context in which our observations are made.

        Thus, such an operation as transitivity, reflects a deep cogni-
tive structure and refers to the competence of the subject to appre-
hend various classes of problems, without necessarily implying that
the individual will demonstrate such understanding in a particular
content. In other words, one may speak of such operations or deep
structures in thought when we see various common properties in the
way in which a solution is achieved, irrespective of the particular
content in which the problem presents itself.

        On the other hand, Krech, Crutchfield, and Ballachey [4] discuss
the nature of a culture and emphasize its technological aspect. It
turns out that whenever technology is an important part of any culture it is only a reflection of that culture's use and discovery of
the objective logical properties of reality - expressed in building a
tepee or in building a rocket. Thus, in spite of the very different
materials employed and the varied cultural influences, we may see
identical logical necessities in the construction of a ship to the
moon or a home on the plains.

        Thus, an understanding of Piaget's developmental point of view
is extremely helpful in understanding both the culture and the behaviors observed. One of the other merits of Piaget's system is that he
has shown that the child is both the creator and the consumer of his
developing cognitive structures. If cognitive structures are taken
as a book, then we may say that the child not only writes the book,
but also reads it. It is in this sense that this "book of knowledge"
is a universal one or not.

THEORETICAL ISSUES

The Framework

        During more than forty years of experimentation, Piaget has
arrived at a formal description of cognitive development and has
divided it into four stages. The first one, before the development
of language (symbolic function) in the child, deals with the construction of the logic of actions. This has been called "the period

of sensorimotor intelligence." Primarily, the process involves the organization of actions into operational patterns, or "schemata of actions," whose main characteristics are to allow the child to differentiate in his actions, between means and goals. Some conditions are necessary in order to achieve this. Space must become organized as a general container; objects must remain permanent; and, in order to anticipate goals, one must assume some acquisition of practical cause processes.

The main consequence of the appearance of the symbolic function is the reorganization of sensorimotor intelligence. This enables the child to integrate symbols, allowing him to expand the range of his operations. This next stage is called "pre-operational," or "the period of egocentric thinking." Thus, from a response to an event, intelligence is mediated through language, but the child is not yet able to maintain in his mind symbols (abstractions) that lead to ideas whose meanings are constant. Those constancies have to do with those aspects of the "real world," such as measure, mass, motion, and logical categories.

In this pre-operational world everything appears to be related to an egocentric point of view. This is a limitation as much as a source of enrichment during this level of intellectual functioning.

The following stage is characterized by the development of concrete operations. From what is essentially a subjective orientation, intellectual functioning moves toward more objectivity in elaborating mental constancies. The child no longer thinks only in terms of himself, but also takes into account the limitations that the external, physical world places upon him. For example, the child no longer believes that the moon follows him down the street. For Piaget, this type of intelligence is called "concrete," because essentially the child is only able to deal with tangible, manipulatable objects. That is, his world is concerned with necessary relations among objects.

The final stage of intellectual development deals with the development of formal thinking which permits the formation not only of necessary relations but also possible and impossible ones. In short, he can "play" with his mind. The child, now an adolescent, can dream things that never were and ask "Why not?" The adolescent is able to make exact deductions, to extract all combinations from a potential or a real situation. He is no longer directed only by concrete relations. He can make hypotheses and elaborate theories. He is able to dissociate the form of his thinking from its content.

We can see then, that Piagetian tests are, of their very nature, hierarchical; they describe a progressive organization, and individual potentialities. They provide a detailed analysis of the functioning of thinking. In short, they qualify thinking, they do not quantify it. They always respect the intelligence of a given child.

Thus, we can describe intelligence functionally; we can formalize its structural development. We cannot assign to intelligence a specific, static definition, for this directly contradicts the idea of development itself.

CROSS-CULTURAL STUDIES

One of the valuable sources of information concerning the "fairness" of Piaget's theory and the validity of the developmental stages is cross-cultural studies. On a theoretical level we may say that the system must be culturally fair because it is involved with a description of a progressive organization directed by logical necessity and thus not greatly influenced by culture, but this does remain an open question. Many cross-cultural studies have been made in the last ten years and some are still in progress. We would like to focus on a few.

Piaget's experiments on conservation and fundamental logico-mathematical concepts have been carried out in Africa, Senegal, Iran, and Algeria. Jerome Bruner [5], for example, has done such work in Senegal.

We want to analyze one example which is illustrated by the study of our colleague, Dr. M. Bovet, from Geneva. Her work was done with Algerian children and its purpose was to study the development of conservation within an almost illiterate population whose ethnic background and cultural values are far removed from Western ones.

Dr. Bovet [6], investigated two distinct cognitive problems: one dealing with the development of physical quantities, such as the conservation of liquid and matter; and the other dealing with elementary metrics, such as conservation of length. The principle of the first experiment is simple: given two equal quantities, A=B (liquid contained in identical containers or matter with identical shape) which are recognized as equal by the child himself, A is poured into a container A' of different dimensions, or A is modelled into a different form. The child is then asked if both quantities are still equal, that is, if A' is still equal to B.

The results obtained demonstrate a development whose sequence follows that of Western children; with some delay in time of acquisition for Algerian children when compared with their European or American counterparts. At 6-7, for example, the Algerian children present the typical reactions observed in pre-operational Western children. They do not believe in invariancy; they maintain that the transformation has changed the quantity of the liquid or the quantity of matter. Alergian children also justify their answers by the same logic as their European peers. A typical reaction is to say that there is more to drink in A' because the level is higher.

For the intermediary stage of oscillation between conservatory and non-conservatory answers, there are no noticible differences except for what concerns the assimilation of external, visible indices. Algerian children seem to be less permeable to perceptual features, and tended to show conservation unless verbal or active behavior on the experimental content was performed. Once the Algerian child was asked to actively act upon the material, or to give a verbal explanation of what had happened, he became absolutely comparable to a European child. For him, as with his Western counterpart, conservation will appear only as a possibility, dependent upon the context, and not as a logical necessity. Around 9-11, the responses are more clearly of an operative nature - the Algerian child believes in conservation and will justify it in the same way that the European child does: "nothing was added during the pouring (transformation), therefore the quantity is equal."

Other cross-cultural studies have been done by Hyde [7] in Aden. A large battery of Piaget's number and quantitative tasks were administered to British, Somali, Arab, and Indian children from 6-7 years of age. The main results are summarized below.

1.   "During the investigation it was a common experience to hear a small Arab, Somali, or Indian child give in Arabic almost a word for word translation of an answer given to the same question by a Swiss child."

2.   The number tasks varied widely in difficulty.

3.   As observed in almost all cross-cultural studies with Piaget's experiments, the notion of stages and their sequence was found to be respected, but there was sometimes a time delay in the age of attainment of a certain stage. It was found that European children performed on a higher genetic level than children of the same age sampled in her study.

One of our concerns was precisely not to limit ourselves to one domain of thinking, but rather to explore three: space, conservation, and elementary logic. This was decided so that we might obtain an overall picture of cognitive development within a particular Non-White ethnic group, rather than a limited view of only one aspect of development. This limited area of focus has been one of the aspects open to criticism of most cross-cultural studies. Thus, our emphasis on spatial notions as well as logical ones reflects an attempt to define a broad area of understanding. We might then find that a time delay in the acquisitions of certain principles in our sample, reflects a general lag in development that we would find in any area examined. On the other hand, we might just as well find that a delay in one area, relative to Geneva norms, is balanced by precisely the reverse situation in another area.

A further point which we would like to make is that one should distinguish between the development of thought as a logical necessity, and the development of thought which depends on environmental stimulation and social mileu. For instance, a European child may use numbers and number concepts much more than notions of space, whereas for an American Indian child, much more emphasis may be placed on space rather than number. In this case, one should not talk simply about who's better on what, but rather emphasize the relative distribution of areas of excellence within an ethnic group.

With respect to the general question of these time delays, it should be pointed out that they present an interesting problem which warrants further examination.

For European children, time delays of all sorts have been described and proven again and again. For example, it is reliably reported that the attainment of conservation of weight always lags behind the attainment of conservation of matter. We thus are faced with the logical problem of understanding why there are such time delays in the equilibration of various aspects of the same general principle, here, conservation.

Interestingly, and perhaps, regrettably, when we find a time delay in a particular area with a particular ethnic group, everyone looks for a logical explanation to explain the gap; whereas when the time delay is between two ethnic groups, everyone seeks a cultural explanation. The paradox is that we too often tend to remain flexible and open in explaining time delays within a White culture, and on the other hand, become rigid and absolute when we judge such delays between two cultures. To make the point explicit, we would caution against prejudice disguised as "scientific fact," when we see that behind it lies unequal standards of comparison.

Disparate Evidence

There have been some studies which appear to give no support at all to Piaget's point of view. We may cite as an example, typical in many respects, the work of Estes [8] on the child's conception of number. We would caution against ready acceptance of her negative results on several grounds. Firstly, her paper is extremely brief and it is not possible to know fully to what her results refer. Secondly, the author does report enough to make it clear that she has not faithfully followed Piaget's means of analysis, and has not really understood the context into which it fits. We may say then that the little disparate evidence that does exist is open to question, but can serve a useful function in pointing to areas of investigation that may require further work.

Epistemological Implications

The epistemological status of cross-cultural studies is clear. If "epistemology" consists in the study of the history of knowledge, and "genetic" refers to its formation during development, we may see a clear relationship between the biological development across phyla, and the mental development across phyla. Piaget points out that if in biology we may loosely say that ontogenesis recapitulates phylogenesis, the same could hold true for mental development. This remains, of course, an open question that must be examined not only by analyzing results within an ethnic group carefully, but also by examining results from different cultural backgrouds. We attempt to do both in our study.

The best approach to the problem of the study of the development of knowledge, would be to study primitive man. If we could turn back the clocks, we might find that the Pithecanthropus possessed a stabilized sensorimotor ability and the beginning of symbolic function. The next human stage logically possessed some pre-operational capacity, and so on, following the phylogenetic stages. Unfortunately, the irreversibility of time forbids us this type of study.

What remains then is a substitution for this type of direct observation and one such substitution would be the cross-cultural study. Another approach now gaining in significance, is the study of thought development through the use of computers - the studies in artificial intelligence [9]. As a matter of fact, the epistemological status of work on how we make computers behave intelligently, as much as the cross-cultural studies, demand a strong emphasis on the need and usefulness of epistemology.

Epistemology is naturally not only knowledge, but also its deep structure and when some years ago, one of the authors published a paper with Papert [10] entitled, "Who needs epistemology." The answer was the engineers who construct machines of intelligence. Cross-cultural studies show in a way how intelligence is engineered.

Another epistemological implication concerns the nature and validity of the stages described. Again, Piaget has described cognitive development as occurring in a sequence of regular stages, each one succeeding its predecessor in logical order, and differing qualitatively from it. We may contrast this with the psychoanalytic point of view, which views the stages in psycho-sexual development as functional rather than structural. This means that in the psychoanalytic notion, any particular stage differs from any other in the prevalence of a certain behavior, rather than in the uniqueness of that behavior. For example, during the oral period, it is not true that we find no phallic behavior but rather, we see mostly oral behavior.

In Piaget's developmental system the existence of a particular stage implies its exclusiveness; the pre-operational child is not mostly pre-operational, he is entirely so. It is a way to see reality which excludes any other way. This difference in the conception of stages is an important one, and has several significant implication. We find, for example, that if we see a pre-operational child who then, is non-conservatory, it is of no use to tell him that the amount of clay to eat in a ball remains constant, no matter the shape, for he thinks us crazy. The fact is that he has a qualitatively different way of viewing the world than an adult does. The implications for education are clear.

Again, the validity of the stages described by Piaget requires careful examination, and are still open to experimental assessment. One interesting area of study would be to understand the way a given concept, such as conservation disappears as we could observe it in psychopathology, but this remains for the future.

A further area of epistemological significance concerns the relationship of thinking and language. Although we do not wish to emphasize linguistic problems, per se, in our work, their relevance will become clear. In this connection, it is interesting to quote Paul Radin [11] in "Primitive Man as Philosopher," when he discusses the relationship of abstract thought and language.

> "What is not so clear, however, to the overwhelming
> majority of scholars and laymen, even if we grant the
> existence of individuals with philosophic interests and the
> capacity of philosophic thinking, is that the languages at
> their disposal were adequate either in structure or in
> vocabulary for the formation of abstract and generalized
> ideas and philosophic concepts. And even if the language
> can be shown to be adequate, many scholars would contend
> that the stage of cultural development reached by abor-
> iginal peoples, to say to least, did not encourage such
> formulations except to a minimal degree." (p xxi).

Thus, Radin demonstrates that primitive man had developed the basic capacities for abstract thought and generalized ideas. It is important to point out though that the formation of such abstractions is not simply an epistemological problem, but also very much refers to the basic processes in logic upon whose structure our present knowledge of the physical and mathematical world was built. It is also important to point out that if one focuses strictly on a structural analysis of language then, it is highly problematical that any meaningful discussion of logical can be made. One could point to some primitive language and through its structural analysis show a basic incapacity for dealing with abstraction.

Similarly, it would be easy to demonstrate that the languages of aboriginal peoples are frequently more complex structurally than are our own that the vocabularies are just as large, sometimes even larger, that words with abstract or generalized connotations are as frequent, indeed, in some native idioms more frequent than in our own, and that the abstract connotation of a word quite commonly is expressed formally by affixes (p xxii). But again, as long as we look only at language structure, we must question how much we really have learned about thinking.

The relevance of this discussion to our present work will soon become clear. Let us go on, for a moment, and note that even people like Cassirer [12] or Lévy-Brühl [13], would make a strong point about the fact that aboriginal peoples do not think abstractly and cannot form generalized concepts because most of their abstract words can be shown to be built up of themes that etymologically possess concrete meanings. There are really two points here which should be clearly made.

1. The first point concerns the origin of logical thinking. Here the problem is wide open. If the assumption of people like Lévy-Brühl is true, that is, that aboriginal people do not think abstractly and perform on a "made of" logic which precludes contradiction, then there is a real problem of understanding the way knowledge can evolve at all. We would like to make the point that an analysis of language alone is not sufficient to understand the nature of logical operations and abstractions, nor is it sufficient to understand the mechanisms of thinking. As Piaget states in his reply [14] to Lévy-Brühl, one has never seen an aborigine confusing a cow and a chair. Explicitly said, the primitive is completely able to make the necessary differentiation and abstractions when he is faced with making sense of the interaction between the "technical" aspect of his world and the logical reflection of this technical aspect. To stretch the point we might imagine that Lévy-Brühl would consider the Sun Dance as a major aspect of Sioux civilization. With his notion of logic of participation, Lévy-Brühl would see the dancer playing the role of the buffalo and maintain that the dancer believes that he is the buffalo himself. For sure though, the actual Sun Dancer does not roam over the plains on his four legs to get to the ceremony, but more likely takes his car! The point here is that he knows perfectly well he is no buffalo.

2. The second point concerns the structure of language. If it is true that there exist universals or deep structures, as Chomsky [15] has stated, then we should not be astonished to find the same structural complexities in primitive languages as in our own. The reason for this parallel complexity lies in the fact that such deep structure is a reflection of basic cognitive operations, and is not a pure linguistic manifestation. In this

connection Radin's point is well taken, and we see a relationship between language and operations, with the operations as primary, since we are unable to understand language alone without referring it to the concrete, physical, technological aspect of a given society.

In other words, the operative aspect of a society strongly implies something which we observe on an ontogenetic level. Again we see support for a notion of the ontogenesis recapitulating a phylogenesis of knowledge. In cognitive development we observe that the basic trend in thinking is towards an integration of contradiction – and this fact seems to remain precisely true on a phylogenetic level. Epistemologically, the only assumption is that man and child have both to deal with a logic of contradiction and that the essential process of knowledge is to solve cognitive conflicts. To do so, what is needed is a logic of order, number, space – a set of operations.

One of the epistemological controversies concerning primitive man and his logic deals with the problem of continuity in phylogenesis. At this point the child's cognitive development is highly enlightening. What we observe during ontogenesis is that both continuity and discontinuity in development exist.

On one hand it is true that the pre-operational child has different structures in thought available to him than the concrete operational child – one proceeds with figurative or perceptual "misleadings," the other with operative transformations. And yet, concrete operations proceed from these same pre-operations. In this sense we see both continuity and discontinuity, for any concrete operational child had to be pre-operational before being operational. This necessarily implies a functional continuity, and in this connection it is not highly pretentious to hypothesize that phylogenetic development follows this same general pattern. Thus, it is useful to draw these parallels between the child's cognitive development and phylogenetic development.

FINAL NOTE

In closing our introduction we should note that the reader will find an explicit description of Piaget's techniques for each experiment that we have used, including features that are not always completely apparent in Piaget's books, such as numbers, percentages of acquisition of the various functions, and Geneva norms. This remark stands for those who feel strongly about repeating these experiments.

II

The Community

The Pine Ridge Reservation lies on the rolling plains of south-western South Dakota in an area not long ago roamed by wild buffalo and brave hunters, but now the home of some 10,000 Oglala Sioux whose largest remaining fight is against widespread illness and abysmal poverty. The reservation is the second largest in the United States, and encompasses some 4,353 square miles of plains, covered by buffalo grass interlaced with creeks, buttes, ravines, and low ridges. The beauty of the reservation--its quiet and open space, the stark still-ness of the Badlands, the primitiveness of the prairie--is also part of its problem, for in its relative isolation and under-development, the reservation can supply meaningful support only to a handful.

The people on Pine Ridge are very poor. Very little of the land is arable and there is little regular work available other than government employment, but even this is sometimes unstable and always open only to a few. Two-thirds of the reservation families have a total yearly income (including welfare) of $3,000 or less, and one in every three families has a total income of less than $1,000 [16]. This is even more striking when we realize that the average Indian family is almost twice as large as the average family in the nation as a whole.

Thus, we see a picture of poverty and illness, isolation and little hope. Erikson [17] points out that this once great nation has been plagued by "an apocalyptic sequence of catastrophies, as if nature and history had united for a total war on their too manly off-spring" [17] (p.116). Let us briefly trace the history of the Oglalas and of Pine Ridge, and then more fully describe what we find today.

26

HISTORICAL SUMMARY

The Dakota Indians (or Sioux, as they have come to be known) are organized into several divisions of which the Teton Dakota are one. There are then seven subdivisions of the Tetons, and the Oglala Sioux represent the largest tribe.

The Teton Dakota are believed to have originated in the south-east and to have begun their migration westward sometime in the 16th century. When by the mid-eighteenth century the Sioux found them-selves in the Black Hills of South Dakota and Wyoming, they soon took great advantage of the plentiful horses and buffaloes, and organized their lives around the hunt of the buffalo. The buffalo's body pro-vided not only food for the nomadic tribes, but also material for clothing and shelter, boats, strings for arrows, fuel, medicine, and ornaments. "Societies and seasons, ceremonies and dances, mythology and children's play extolled his name and image" [17] (p.116).

By the mid-nineteenth century, however, hordes of White people in an endless flow of covered wagons, streamed into the plains. With the Whites came conflict and disease, and ultimately the wanton de-struction of the buffalo. By the early 1870's, attempts were already being made to confine the Ogalas to reservation life and encourage their active involvement in agriculture. To the traditional Sioux hunter, this was women's work and thus such plans were doomed to fail. Further reason for hoping the Sioux could be conveniently con-fined to an area which would be of little use to others, came with the discovery of gold in the Black Hills of South Dakota. This region was a sacred land for the Sioux and was expressly protected from White incursion by a treaty entered upon with the government.

The Government first offered to pay for the Hills, but when this was not easily arranged, a detachment under General Custer was sent to drive the Sioux into their agencies, with force if necessary. Custer underestimated the strength and determination of the bands led by Crazy Horse, Sitting Bull, Gall, Black Moon and Big Road; and his confidence of spring 1876 was quickly reversed at the Little Big Horn in June of that year. With Custer finished, the Sioux wanted only to return to peaceful hunting, but the government was not soon to forget that battle. For the next ten or fifteen years the Sioux were hounded constantly by the U.S. military, and increasing pressure was brought upon them to settle permanently at designated agencies. Fighting went on not only between the government and the Indian, but also among Indians, as the tribal political and power system was strained to the limit.

The Sioux were unhappy but not yet resigned to reservation life. They longed for the return of the freedom of the past and were ready to try anything to insure its return. It was in 1889 that the people at Pine Ridge Agency first heard of the teachings of Wavoka - the Messiah - a man from the west who had received a wonderful revel-ation.

If the Indian people would subscribe to this new religion and its central Ghost Dance, a new day would come in which happiness would return and the people would ultimately be reunited in heaven with all of their dead friends and relatives. The Oglalas further believed that with adherence to Wavoka's teachings, the White man would be banished and the buffalo would return in plenty to the plains [18].

The growing acceptance of the Ghost Dance Religion was met with a growing concern among the Whites, and to the new government agent at Pine Ridge, dancing Indians meant trouble; ironically, one of the basic tenets of the new religion was peacefulness, and yet, in response to the growing zeal with which the religion was followed, the new agent mustered his troops for combat.

Thus, on the morning of December 29, 1890, a detachment of the same Seventh Cavalry that had some years before been represented by Custer in Montana, sought to meet and disarm a band of Sioux under Chief Big Foot, at Wounded Knee on the Pine Ridge Reservation. Although historians disagree somewhat as to detail, it is known that a shot rung out which prompted the cavalry, with its artillery carefully aimed at tepees of men, women, and children, to begin the slaughter which signaled the end of the Indian wars with the US forces.

When the smoke cleared, infants were found frozen to death near their wounded and now dead mothers; men, women, and children, some 183 of them, had been "quieted" by the troops. But the tragedy at Wounded Knee scored far deeper than a simple death toll can tell, for it was the death of the hope that the old days would return and that the traditional life could continue. It was "the climax to and the symbol of the loss of spirit of a once proud people"[16] (p.43). The Oglalas had uttered their last warlike breath in the struggle with the invading White men, and settled, somewhat distrustingly, on reservation life and the government promise of support.

The history of the last seventy or eighty years at Pine Ridge is probably marked more than anything else by the lack of a clear or uniform government policy towards the people of the reservation, and the failure of the emergence of any effective Indian leaders to organize and make known the people's wishes. The making of history has been left to a rather "arbitrary succession of representatives who had one or another ... objectives in mind - thus demonstrating an inconsistency which the Indians interpreted as insecurity and bad conscience" [17] (p.117).

For the first 20 years of this century the government literally kidnapped children from the reservation and sent them away to government schools. Their hair was shaven, the use of the native tongue, Lakota, was forbidden, and the practice of Indian rituals and maintenance of Indian crafts was not permitted. The government attempted to "civilize" the red man, but by this did nothing more than rob him of his ways, and offer nothing in replacement.

During this time, it was only the role of the cowboy which inspired the Indian. But Washington, in 1917, bowed to the pressures of White cattlemen, and forbade the Indian from using reservation land for this purpose. Then followed a period in which the Sioux were encouraged to farm their arid land, but only little of the reservation allotment could realistically be so used, and farming was foreign to the Sioux people of recent times anyway.

There are no longer soldiers at Pine Ridge, but the years of disappointment and poor planning have left the people distrustful and yet dependent. The Indian today, has little trust in the government and often, less trust in himself. To be sure, he has been wronged and is owed much by the government both legally and morally.

PINE RIDGE TODAY

It is with this perspective that we must view the descendants of the proud hunter and the defeated warrior today. For to lose sight of history, one would of necessity lose any sense of the future - and it is with the latter that we are basically committed.

Today we see the reservation as in many ways cut-off and isolated from the rest of society. There is no bus or train service connecting it with the outside world, and an air-strip has just now been built for use by government personnel. Similarly, there is no public transportation system connecting points within the reservation, and of the 530 miles of reservation roads only 150 are hard surfaced, and thus travel is difficult in bad weather. Two-thirds of the Indian households have a car or truck, but for the family without some vehicle, transportation presents a real problem. Similarly, the communications network is poor, and while most families own a radio, the availability of a variety of programing is very much limited. Until very recently there was no local newspaper, and the first edition of a four-page weekly has just appeared.

The Pine Ridge Reservation is 74% Indian, and this group is comprised of 52% Mixed Blood and 48% Full Blood [16]. This distinction is more than one of blood quantum, for one sees differences in the degree to which contemporary middle-class values are embraced; moreover, there is a good deal of division squabbling between these groups.

Of the inhabitants of Pine Ridge, some 50% live in small villages, while 35% live in isolated houses in the country and 15% live in rural clusters of three or four houses. With respect to language preference among Indians, in 32% of the households only English is spoken, in 9% mostly English, in 44% both English and Lakota are spoken equally, in 10% mostly Lakota is spoken, and in 5% of the households only Lakota is spoken. While the use of Lakota seems to be declining somewhat among Mixed-Bloods, the native tongue has been fairly consistently used among Full-Bloods.

It is interesting to note that the Pine Ridge population is an extremely youthful one, the median age among Indians being 16.7 years. Among reservation Indians, almost 2/3 of the population is under 25 years of age and over 1/2 is under 18. One critical implication of these statistics is that unless meaningful measures are taken to provide better education and service, the social and economic problems on the reservation will worsen as these young people grow older.

And indeed, the present economic situation is striking. Almost 2/3 of Indian households report a total annual income (including welfare) of less than $3,000. Only 1/3 of the working force is employed and of this, some 25% are employed only part-time. Among the full-time employed, 13% have only temporary jobs, and among the part-time employed, 73% are only temporarily employed. It is clear then that although the total unemployment rate is strikingly 10 times higher than the national average, this tends strongly to underestimate the actual picture.

Thus, less than 1/4 of all Indians have a totally earned income; some 40% have a totally unearned income; 21% have both earned and unearned income, and some 14% have no income whatever. Whatever employment is available is generally unstable and often of low status. It is not surprising then that as one travels from district to district he sees not simply sub-standard living conditions, but rather deplorable conditions for contemporary America. About half of the Indian homes have only one or two rooms, only 40% of them have an inside source of water, and only 40% of Full-Blood homes and 81% of Mixed-Blood homes have electricity. Maynard and Twiss [16] conclude that the present social and economic conditions render the people of Pine Ridge one of the most underprivileged in the country. It is with this total environment that the reader should be acquainted.

III

Child Rearing — Formal Education

It is clear that practices of child rearing and the nature of the home environment in general have great influence upon the process of formal education. What is not so clear, however, is a simple picture of these early years. However, again referring to the valuable work of Maynard and Twiss [16] there are certain general trends that can be found.

Although we find that affect is not easily expressed between Indian people in general, it is the very young and the very old for whom exceptions are readily made. Family and friends meet the newborn with happiness and excitement, and love is lavished upon them. Infant care is largely in the hands of the mother and the first several years of the child's life are fairly uncomplicated and generally permissive.

Full-Blood children tend to be more shy and retiring than do Mixed-Bloods, especially toward White strangers. One thing which is very much the same between groups though, is the great deal of freedom typically given the child in the first years of life.

When school age comes though, one notes a decrease in the open display of feelings from parent to child. Affection is now more often expressed in the giving of gifts, and the value of generosity is instilled early in a child. During this period the child grows increasingly away from the home as the locus of all activity.

Discipline now becomes of more concern to parents, and while the Mixed-Blood parent generally applies a fair measure of praise or scolding to make his direction known, the more traditional Full-Blood parent may praise his child for something well done but tends to

31

apply the force of shame to counteract and correct a child gone wrong. One often observes though that in either case the spoken word may not be followed by meaningful action and the child may go on as he pleases.

In this relatively permissive atmosphere one might expect the emergence of great independence and self-direction amongst the growing youth. This however, does not seem to be true. Rather, we see in adolescence, perhaps a too large measure of insecurity, passivity, dependence, and depression. It is in this context that we may see the teenager increasingly withdraw into apathy and non-participation, turn away from school and perhaps towards anti-social behavior. The Indian adolescent tends to have low aspirations, and this grows both from a negative self-image and the realities of his immediate environment.

EDUCATION AND FORMAL LEARNING

With respect to formal education, today on the reservation there are three independent school systems, the Federal schools of the Bureau of Indian Affairs, the public schools of the various counties, and the parochial system of the Roman Catholic Church. Taken together, the reservation has a total of twenty-six grammar schools and three high schools with a total enrollment of about 4400 Indian and White children and 227 teachers.

There are problems, though, in education on the reservation. Fully 27% of the youngsters in school are at least 2 years older than the normal age for their grade. Over 80% of the people now 25 years or older have not completed high school. More than 70% of the children completing the eighth grade will drop out before finishing high school, and about half this number actually drop out before completing the ninth grade. Over 1/5 of the present population of 16 year olds has already dropped-out of school. Table 1 gives a quick summary of the educational level of people now 25 and over, for Pine Ridge residents, and the nation as a whole.

Thus, the educational level of the reservation Indian falls significantly below that of the total US population. The average reservation Indian has completed 8.7 years of school, while the average for White America is 12.0 years.

To what can we attribute the relative lowering of academic success amongst the Pine Ridge population?

This question is certainly not easily answered, and is one which we raise now, only to return again later. It would seem that one aspect of this high rate of underachievement is the result of a lack of sufficient motivation to do well.

Table 1. (after Maynard and Twiss, p.73): Educational
Level of the Reservation Population as Compared to US White
and Negro Populations - for Persons 25 Years and Older.

Years of School Completed	Reservation		US Population	
	Indian	White	Negro	White
8th Grade or less	56%	28%	50%	31%
1-3 years of high school	25%	15%	22%	18%
4 years of high school	15%	31%	18%	32%
1-3 years of college	3%	11%	5%	9%
4 or more years of college	1%	15%	5%	10%

To be sure, the parents of school-age children, and the youngsters themselves, see school as the key to vocational success. Many
feel that without school one can never achieve self-respect and independence, yet paradoxically the belief persists that staying in
school is a waste of time [19]. Behind this sense of hopelessness,
the Indian youth feels inferior and powerless and as these convic-
tions grow, so declines success in school.

Furthermore, inspite of the typical parent's sense that school
should be attended, there is a passivity with respect to personal involvement in school matters which often may look like disinterest in
the education of their children. These parents are often far too
pressured by more basic and immediate needs, and they seem content to
leave education in the hands of others who claim competence [19], and
hope that the job will get done.

In the classroom, itself, there persist certain cultural bar-
riers between teacher and pupil which also serve to lower a young-
ster's desire to remain. For example, it is difficult for many
educators to appreciate the effects of the still-prevalent cultural
value which holds that one member of the group should not try to
stand out above others.

A student who strives for a high level of accomplishment is
often ridiculed by his peers, and the net result is a great leveling
effect wherein only extremely few will allow themselves to strive for
excellence in school. Too often we may find a "cultural and linguistic gulf between teacher and pupils, augmented by the great social
distance between federal employees and Indian parents and augmented
further by the bewildering impact of a curriculum supposed to render
the children socially more acceptable (to a small town or lower
middle-class milieu) which creates a situation in which the teacher
finds herself with virtually no influence over the peer society
(children of the classroom)" [19](p.114). Thus, cultural influences,

a sense of futility, and unstable home and family conditions all contribute to a picture of poor school adjustment and low achievement.
To complete the vicious circle, we note that too many educators
expect little from their Indian pupils, and thus further insure that
they will get little. Much evidence has already been produced which
clearly indicates that the quality of a student's performance is very
much affected by what his teacher believes he can do. In this way,
poor performance further re-erates poor performance.

There is a distinctly positive side to the outlook on education
as well. When we think of formal learning we too often think only of
the academic staff of school. However, we note that the moral aspect
of learning is just as important in education as is the addition of
new knowledge.

In this connection we still see many examples in contemporary
Oglala life which reflect the central importance of moral judgement
to the traditional Sioux. We may examine, as an example, the Sun
Dance, once again performed every summer at Pine Ridge.

Traditionally, the practice of the Sun Dance was of great
significance amongst the Sioux, being of both deeply religious and
social importance. It was the occasion on which people would gather
to give thanks or, in special cases, to seek power from the Great
Spirit. It is significant that in the old days, and to some measure
today too, the sun dancer could only participate by virtue of his
possession of the four great traits: bravery, generosity, fortitude,
and integrity.

While some might argue that the Sun Dance has lost much of its
religious significance and that many no longer take it seriously,
this is really not the point. What is important though is that these
values have long been identified with the Sioux and are still considered of great significance.

Thus, bravery, generosity, fortitude, and integrity are not
taught at school, but yet constitute a great part of Indian education. Piaget [20] in his book on moral judgements in children and
later Kohlberg [21] strongly make the point that the achievement of
reciprocity in moral judgement - the ability to understand and reflect upon moral issues, both with respect to the self and others -
comes only at one of the last stages of cognitive development and is
usually associated with the presence of formal thinking. Here at
Pine Ridge, reciprocity in terms of generosity, and sharing constitutes one of the important aspects of common life. In this sense we
must understand that the identification with such a value system formally implies a high level of thinking. When we consider problems in
the development of the abilities to think, we need consider more than
reading, writing, and arithmetic.

IV

The Pine Ridge Development Study: Formal Approach

RATIONALE

In order to get a fair idea of cognitive development within a population, one may proceed in at least two ways. The first, which we may call the quantitative approach, demands that we see many subjects so that precise numerical results may be obtained. With this the case, it is under usual circumstances necessary to examine only a limited area of study, for to seek a broad base of experimentation would be an enormous task. The obvious sacrifice made in this approach is that it is often difficult and sometimes impossible to gain a real understanding of a generalized pattern of thought when a strictly quantitative approach is used, for we have examined only a limited area.

With the second approach, which is essentially qualitative in nature, one attempts to get an overall picture of the development of various basic domains of thought. In this connection, we emphasize the genetic aspect of research rather than the quantitative. In fact, this is the main thrust of our research and we have sought to cover much developmental ground and thus gain an overall picture. We have then chosen three basic areas for study: the basic invariancies, concepts of space, and elementary logic. Let us first say a few words about these areas of thought, and then return to our rationale for their selection.

As a brief summary, we may say that within cognitive development we can distinguish at least two basic processes, these being the development of logical and infra-logical operations. The logical processes deal with classifications and relations of order, with entire objects whose position in space is of no importance. Thus the

35

logical processes are discontinuous and from them develop concepts of number.

The infra-logical processes, on the other hand, deal with notions of space, time, and speed, and thus deal with continuous properties whose placement in space is important. From the infra-logical processes grow concepts of measure.

In our experiments we deal with the logical operations through the development of classification - class inclusion, and the development of ordering relations - seriation. Infra-logical operations are dealt with through our experiments with geometrical drawings and landscape rotation.

Underlying the development of these logical and infra-logical processes, is the development of concepts of permanence and invariance. Thus, until the child can remove himself from solely considering the perceptual attributes of a problem, he cannot offer an abstract point of view. In our work we deal with these invariances and conservation in two realms, continuous and discontinuous. For continuous properties we use conservation of liquid, matter, and weight; for discontinuous properties, conservation of number and length, and the 1:1 correspondence.

Let us now return to our rationale for selection of these experiments, for it is good to point out the importance of assuming the various areas of thought.

We might note, for example, that when Piaget talks about the characteristics of the concrete operational level of thinking, he assesses general characteristics like the acquisition of conservation, of reversibility, the relationship of these concrete operations to concrete manipulations, the mastery of simple logical operations like classifications, relations, number, space and measure. To understand the period of concrete operations, or any period for that matter, one must consider the interlacing of a variety of functions.

In this respect, there exists a misunderstanding about the very nature of the concrete operational period of thinking. For example, in one of our studies [22] we showed that in the domain of time, the pre-operational child is able to perform certain rudimentary or semi-operational processes. The problem was as follows: the child sees two trains, one of which travels twice as fast as the other. Each train has two possible pathways along which it may travel, and thus the young child can adjust the distance covered by each. The child at this stage may adjust the pathway of the faster train, such that it now has twice the distance to travel as the slower train. Thus, he can compensate for a greater rate by an increase in distance, yet if he is asked if both trains have spent the same amount of time in going from their respective origins to their points of terminus, he will insist that the faster train on the longer path has spent more time in its travel. In this case he is caught by the greater distance and cannot modify his thought with reference to a proportionally greater speed.

Here is the point. Controversy arises when one wants to discuss what is really meant by the acquisition of the concrete operational period of thinking. For if we limited ourselves only to consideration of the instance when the child makes an adjustment of distance, when he makes a type of operational adjustment, we would say that he has achieved an operational level of thought, but if we limit ourselves to the situation in which he maintains that the longer pathway always takes more time to traverse, no matter the speed, we must say he has not achieved operational thought as yet.

Thus, much controversy will remain as long as we limit ourselves to one aspect of thinking. The same point holds true for the origin of conservation. While Bruner [23] holds that the origin of conservation comes from the singular notion of identity ("It's the same amount of clay as before - shape doesn't matter - you didn't add any or take any away"), Piaget [24] strongly disagrees. The rationale for the choice of our experiments rests implicitly in this controversy. For what does it mean to be a concrete operation child? Strictly, on a psychological level, Piaget states that the concrete operational child has undergone a restructuring and reorganizing of his thoughts which have previously depended on actions. Thus, operations are the result of a mechanism of differentiation coming from physical experiences and logico-mathematical experiences. In other words, an operation is an abstraction which leads to the discovery of fundamental properties among objects like the properties of invariance, reversibility, and so on.

On the other hand, from a logical point of view, Piaget states that the concrete operational period of thinking could be characterized by laws of totalities. Thus, we find a logical order which has four properties:

(a) direct composition (2+4=6)
(b) reversibility (6-2=4; once I have added I can subtract)
(c) identity (3+0=0+3)
(d) associativity [(3+1)+2+3+(1+2)]

Thus, Piaget's psychological and logical points of view lead to a criticism sometimes leveled at him. When he formally describes some aspect of behavior in logical terms he is accused by his psychological peers of being a logicist. On the other hand, the logician concerned with abstract formalizations accuses Piaget of psychologism. We should not that the truth of the matter is that any good formalization which seeks to render a generalized picture of the levels of thinking must be consistent with the behaviors observed. Furthermore, Piaget takes the precaution of talking of an epistemic subject in development. He recognizes that since a formalization is itself an abstraction, when speaking formally one would be relatively unable to speak of an individual in particular. When we spoke of the epistemological implications in our introduction, this was also one of our concerns.

The epistemological subject is really the summary of the behavior of many subjects, describing the passage of a consistent series of stages through development. Such constitute the main basis for our talking of a structure of thinking. Thus, in designing our present research with the intent of examining many areas of cognition, we were really getting at two points. One concern was to analyze the acquisition of the developmental stages in various realms, to be then compared to our norms for Geneva. Secondly, we hoped to validate the very notion of stages itself, for with the awareness that we can never talk of an isolated operation but only of an interlacing of operations, it becomes clear that the very fact that we could observe such operations or not - not in one given realm but in general - tends to validate the idea of stages itself?

Piaget constantly emphasizes the idea that the operations stand together and form a whole structure or totality. This means that an isolated operation is never sufficient to assess a stage of development. But what is really meant by an operation?

The term "operation" is a very basic one for an understanding of Piaget. In his book "Six Psychological Studies" alone, it appears approximately once on each page, as if this term underlies the whole theory. As a matter of fact, it does. Piaget [25] defines an operation as follows:

"An operation is, in effect, an internalized action which
has become reversible and coordinated with other operations
in a grouping governed by the laws of the system as a
whole. To say that an operation is reversible is to say
that every operation corresponds to an inverse operation,
as is true, for example, for logical or arithmetic addition
and subtraction..." [25] (p. 121)

THE FOUR CONDITIONS OF AN OPERATION

It is an Action

As a matter of fact, in order to speak of an operation, we ought to have four conditions fulfilled. First it has to be an action. For instance, to reunite two classes of objects into a new class (men plus women is equal to human species) is an action that we can perform mentally but that the child performs at the beginning in a concrete, material way before interiorizing it under the form of a mental or symbolic operation.

It is Interiorizable

This brings us to the second condition: an operation is an interiorizable action. The child may learn arithmetical operations, but he only really understands them in manipulating the objects. Later, these arithmetical operations will interiorize themselves under generalized and abstract forms which abstract any kind of object, as is done in pure mathematics.

In other words, the development, for instance, of mathematical notions can be conceived along three distinct levels, separated in time but functionally related: on a first level, the child simply manipulates, acts with real concrete objects. There may be stones, which he puts together. On a second level, he will be able to use any object, a relation that he has abstracted from one particular experience. This form of abstraction remains concrete because it is still related to given content. (Piaget calls this type of intelligence concrete because it deals with real objects, and operation because it used essentially operations resulting from this first form of abstraction.) On a third level, the child can abstract any kind of object and use it in any sort of logico-mathematical problem situation. That is to say, he will use the abstraction itself as a new property and a new operation. This form of abstraction Piaget will call formal, because it dissociates the form from any given content, the possible from the necessary. For this reason this third level of intelligence is called formal.

It is Reversible

Does this description mean that any action will be an operation? No, because we still have to mention two other conditions, which are necessary in order for us to speak of an operation. To become an operation, an action has not only to be interiorizable, it has also to be reversible, that is to say that it can be performed in either direction. For instance, we can add but we can also subtract. We can reunite but also dissociate. That already means that every action is not reversible. Smoking a cigarette is not a reversible action because we cannot smoke the same cigarette twice.

But if we pour water from a cup A into a cup B, we can pour it back. In this case our action is reversible. This notion of reversibility if a fundamental one. It allows us to think because it is a necessary condition for us in order to relate an initial state to a final one.

Reversibility is directly related to the idea of invariance or conservation. In a fundamental sense, without reversibility we would have no conservation and reciprocity. We would be unable to distinguish a transformation from one state to another. Hence we have to understand what has remained constant during a transformation in order to understand not only the transformation itself but also the states themselves. Since a transformation is really an operation, and since the states are related to each other by the transformations themselves, it follows that the states are dependent upon the transformation. This point has many consequences and implications.

For example, it we present to a child a glass of particular width and height, half filled up (A) and another empty glass (B) thinner but taller than A, we will call state (S1) the situation in which A is filled up and B is empty and (S2) the next state in which B is filled and A is empty. On the other hand, we will call the transformation (T) the pathway from one state to another, that is to say, in this particular case, the pouring from A to B as well as the change of level S2 since it is taller than in S1. For the child to understand these two aspects of the transformation, he must be able to understand the operation of conservation because this operation is precisely the process which has transformed one state to another. On the other hand, the knowledge of the state themselves is only a description of the observable.

That is how and why Piaget distinguishes between these two aspects of thinking: (a) the figurative aspect, which deals with the description of the states and concerns perception; (b) the operative aspect, which provides the understanding of the pathway from A to B. Before having built the adequate logical operations the child thinks only in terms of the states and hence in an essentially figurative or pre-operational way. So, when we pour the water from glass A into glass B, the five-year-old child will say that we have more to drink because the level is higher. He does not yet grasp conservation. He only compares the initial configuration to the final one. He does not relate them in an operational way. He observes that the level has changed and makes the conclusion that the quantity itself must have changed. Accordingly he relies on some perceptual features which are not relevant in order to evaluate presence or absence of conservation. Such a child is called pre-operational precisely because he does not possess the ability to use true reversibility. When he has understood the meaning of the reversible action, he will use it and say: "The quantity did not change; we can pour it back. It is taller but it is also thinner." That is to say that he will think in an operational way in terms of the transformations.

It is Part of a Total Structure

There is a fourth and last important condition of existence of an operation: we never have an isolated operation but an operation is always interdependent on other operations.

The idea then of a total structure means that the child will perform consistently, no matter the content. The "good" operation will be used. On the concrete operational level he is no more misled by the figurative aspect of thinking, and hence is able to perform operatively in a general sense.

For instance, in conservation he will no longer believe that the height of a column of liquid alone determines its amount as it is poured from one size container to another. In elementary logic he will no more have difficulty with the extension and comprehension of a class, and therefore when he sees more horses than lions in front of him he will no longer say there are more horses than animals. In seriation he will no more see the ten sticks as unrelated and therefore each of them having a perceptually unrelated existence. In space he will no longer be misled by the 1:1 correspondence of his spatial arrangement and the examiner's but will work on the necessary transformations in order to establish a logically good configuration, and so on.

So our broad approach to several areas of thought has had a deep rationale. Although the several experiments focus on different logical realms, at the same time they strongly underscore this property of a total structure, which is implied by the concrete operational period of thinking. Also, because the logical similarities of all stress the idea of a total structure rather than some particular achievement in one particular logical realm, we are lead to the following statement of hypotheses:

1   Given the ethnic group under study and recognizing that the standard tests have assessed relative inferiorities in achievement, can we expect that these inferiorities reflect some delay in the most fundamental and basic processes in the development of thinking?

2   If we indeed find that the stages are respected in their sequence then we open our side to a crucial criticism. One could argue that if we do find a super-imposition between data for White and Indian children, then Piaget's tests are not sensitive enough to show differences. This is precisely why we were cautious in choosing a broad base of tests. For, in selecting a whole range of tests and finding in each of them a succession of stages comparable to Geneva, we have demonstrated the independence of operatory development from cultural bias, and indicated their basic nature. Thus, if we find the same succession of stages in each realm when we examine the results cross-culturally, we may say that Piaget's tests are indeed more sensitive than the standard tests. Piaget's tests are precisely meant to be culture-fair and are meant to assess cognitive development. Our question then is, is it true or not that Piaget's tests are more basic than some other tests?

3   Concerning the rate of development, cross-cultural studies show
        that although we may observe an identical stage development, we
        sometimes find a relative time delay in the acquisition of cer-
        tain operations, when we examine the results between cultures.
        Would it be possible to find, instead of a delay, an advance in
        the attainment of certain operations in some different ethnic
        background which would be related to the way of life rather than
        the trend of development? In other words, although the stages
        are respected, the time of their acquisition may vary. This does
        not question the logic of stages, but simply the particular time
        of acquisition of some notion.

4   The fourth hypothesis concerns the relationship between language
        and cognition. Again, although we did not basically address
        ourselves to this problem, there are some aspects of the Lakota
        language which allow us to consider this type of question that
        Furth [26] and others have considered.

        For example, Lakota has no verbal form defining a past or future
        tense; the context in which the verb appears connotes the tense.
        In other words, it is rather a language of the present. Further,
        it is a well known fact [27] that logical classification are
        favored by language. It seems also almost common knowledge that
        spatial operations are related to the ability to differentiate
        coordinates in time - to make statements about a past and
        future. Thus, at a first glance one could argue that a cultural
        group whose language does not facilitate spatio-temporal differ-
        entiation would have a parallel difficulty in dealing with
        spatial organization. We might expect that for this group the
        ability to make differentiations in a spatial world would be
        acquired relatively later in development, since its language
        does not favor this development. However, if this hypothesis
        happens not to be true, that is, if we do not happen to observe
        such a time delay, then we have illustrated the following point:

            Abilities such as classification, seriation, and spatial
            coordination would then seem to be relatively dependent upon
            an origin which is neither perceptual nor linguistic, but as
            Piaget states it [27] in "The Early Growth of Logic in the
            Child," dependent upon early sensorimotor activities - from
            the child's actions themselves.

        This means that if we find no such time delay and our results
        conform to those found in Geneva, then we have suggested that
        the origin of operations is in sensorimotor actions.

        Furthermore, in a study in Geneva by Sinclair de Zwart [28],
        the relationship between conservation, seriation, and language
        was specifically studied. Sinclair, before becoming convinced of
        Piaget's point of view, happens to have been one of his strong

opponents in her belief that language was one of the main factors in the development of thinking. In her work she tried very hard to give the child verbal training to help him learn conservation and seriation. The result was not very encouraging for a point of view which held that language is the principal factor in the development of thinking. For sure, it helps, but it is not everything.

Concern about the role of language in the acquisition of operations grew some time ago, by the following troubling fact. An experiment was performed to investigate the development of the notion of identity.

Liquid in one container is subsequently poured into a series of different containers of varying shape. At each point the child is asked if it is the same liquid, if its nature has changed, etc. One child was observed who spontaneously offered the three arguments for conservation as a response: (a) "you can pour it back and see it's the same," (b) "you didn't add any or take any away," (c) "this glass is taller than the first but it is also thinner." He concluded by saying that, nevertheless, there remained more to drink in one glass than when it was in another.

This was interesting because although the child did not conceptually possess conservation, he could verbally supply all the necessary reasons for explaining why conservation should be true. It was felt that he must have gone through some learning experiment in which an attempt was made to teach conservation, and indeed this turned out to be true.

When the child described in more detail the conservation experiment through which he had passed (in a later section we will describe in detail the conservation experiments that we have applied), he expressed a further interesting point. He noted not only that when a quantity of liquid is in a tall skinny glass it has more to drink than when it is in a shorter glass (more to drink: greater height), but that, in fact, the quantities of liquid were never really the same but it was only when there was an obvious difference in the containers that this became apparent.

Thus, returning to our point, when he was given a relatively simpler task (the identity problem is an easier one than the conservation problem), he applied what had been previously verbally mastered and was then forced to say that the liquids A, and A2 were never the same, to maintain consistency. It is clear that he had been unable to establish a functional relationship between his verbal argument and the operation implied. It is important to remember that one can maintain a good verbal argument and still not possess the necessary operations in thought.

5   In two experiments in particular we took the liberty of changing
the usual procedure so that we might additionally get information on learning abilities. We then compare spontaneous
achievements with final achievement after having used a learning
strategy. One of these experiments was related to spatial
abilities, the other to elementary logic. Although we were not
interested in the assessment of the capacity to learn one particular notion, we were interested in the individual ability to
learn from the situation itself.

Barbel Inhelder [29] in a translated study performed some 20
years ago, was able to draw relevant implications from a type of
Piagetian learning situation, for the diagnosis of mental retardation. In her conclusions she makes three points, which are
based upon experiments in conservation with a population of
mental retardates.

   - She found almost a total analogy between the thinking of her
   subjects and the ego-centrical mentality of young children.
   - There existed a precise parallel between normal and mentally
   retarded children, in both the mechanisms of construction and
   the integration of concepts of conservation, but the mentally
   retarded child did show certain fixations in thinking which
   did not allow for a final equilibration, a final resolution,
   of the tasks presented.
   - She observed a para-normal vacillation between different
   levels of cognitive construction, and noted the effect of
   social exchange on the fragility of intellectual operations in
   mental debility.

Concerning the second point, one of the clinical features of
mental retardation is precisely the inability to learn from
experience, and in changing our technique, we wanted roughly to
assess this point. Furthermore, the type of information the
child is able to integrate and the level on which he can do so,
tells us much about his learning strategy. It is feasible that
the pre-operational child will integrate local learning but will
be unable to perform a generalized learning. Thus, we will also
observe changes in the strategy of learning, through cognitive
development.

Thus, we make two points. We first attempt to assess individual
potentialities to integrate a particular kind of learning. We
also seek to understand the relationship between different modes
of learning and the stage of cognitive development.

On the other hand, one of the striking results of learning
experiments like those of Wohlwill [30], Bruner [31], and
Smedslund [32], for example, is that they have shown that the
pre-operational child is unable to change his point of view

about conservation one iota, while those subjects who are already vacillating do show such a capacity and may move towards conservation. Our joy should be tempered by the fact that no learning works for children who are convinced that the figurative or perceptual aspect of the world is the most basic. They therefore are unable to deduce an abstracted notion like conservation, from even a well planned learning procedure. A vacillating subject, however, is able to vacillate towards an operational answer under such a learning condition, but he probably would actually take this course anyway, even without a learning procedure. This really says much about how teaching and learning must proceed.

What we have tried to do in this case is to focus on an initial question about learning which is the relation between a strategy to integrate information and the particular level of thinking at which it occurs. Is it inconsistent to think that a pre-operational child cannot accomplish a generalized learning but only a very local learning? If it is true that such children can only show local learning, then this would parallel what we find in many other instances where we observe that the pre-operational child shows a compensation between space and time, but not a compensation in a general sense. Therefore, we are reluctant to speak of our work in this connection as a learning experiment, but are eager to talk of an experiment dealing with consistent modes of integration of information. This work, on one hand enlightens a child's capacity, and then too, points to another property of a given stage in development.

In short, the problem of learning takes on another dimension here, and this is the dimension of the particular stage in which the child is and his consequent ability to integrate information by one mode or another. Here we focus on the structure - the mode of learning. The hypothesis concerns learning ability and the child's organizational structure.

6   The final hypothesis deals with specific achievements for particular notions, and the question of time delays that are observed between two ethnic groups. There are two areas of interest here (a) we seek to evaluate the consistency of achievement within one logical realm, such as conservation. Our interest is in discovering if we do get the same type of time delays within a particular logical realm as have been observed elsewhere. Also (b) we would like to compare achievements between logical realms and between two ethnic groups. For example, we might find that the Oglala child could perform well in an area like space, relative to his European peer, and not quite as well as a European child in an area like conservation. If such should be the case, then one should be cautious in his interpretation. That is, if we do find disparities in the relative

distribution of areas of excellence, we might gain greater understanding of the way in which logical notions get built upon each other.

POPULATION

It was thus with the conviction that one could learn much about the development and potential of thinking through the approach of Piaget, for more than with static measures of "reading, writing, and arithmetic," that we came to Pine Ridge. Long before we set foot on the reservation, however, much groundwork had been laid for our program.

Under the supervision of the Acting Director of the Community Mental Health Program and with the aid of staff members, a series of community meetings was organized in which our research proposal and its implications were discussed. Such meetings were held with both educators and administrators of various government agencies, and with the parents of potential participants in our study.

At this initial phase there were, interestingly, two levels of objection. Those educators who offered resistance seemed concerned with a proposal of some new and different method for accomplishing what they knew well to do: evaluating their own pupils. We have suggested that the use of such time-tested techniques as the Stanford-Binet test of intelligence might need re-examining; there was a good deal of discussion and some measure of proselytizing which had to be done. It finally became clear though, that our approach might be of value in offering a different kind of information about the school population, and the cooperation of the government personnel was thus enlisted.

The meetings with parents prompted a different form of objection, and probably one which was more significant. The people of Pine Ridge have over the years been studied, surveyed, questionnaired, tested, evaluated, and "understood" by many who have come and gone leaving the community none the wiser. They felt that too much research had already been done by too many researchers who cared more for their own publications than for feeding information back to the community. With this point we were in strong agreement and it could not be stressed enough that our basic conviction was that the greatest value of our work must be for the community.

Through such meetings a series of lists of potential participants was drawn. Principals from several reservation schools each submitted some 10-20 names of children registered in their schools, for inclusion in our work. The only criterion which we set was that a specified number of children at each age level from 4 through 10 years be selected. To the best possible informal control, the children were selected without concern with any special problems or abilities. From these lists we ultimately selected the children we would see and this was (for our normal population) without any knowledge of these children.

We arrived at Pine Ridge then, with much administrative work already under way. It was then our task to continue meeting with parents and school people who had expressed interest in our work, for the purpose of drawing up plans for seeing the children and securing parental permisssion. Special thanks again goes to Mr. Marvin Roscow and the co-author Mrs. Gayla Twiss for their support during this phase of the work.

Although at first it was planned to sample children from all over the reservation, it was now decided that for practical reasons it would be best to limit our sampling to three districts. Our population then is drawn from White Clay, Wakpamni, and Wounded Knee Districts and consists of 71 children from 4 through 10 years of age.

In Wakpamni District we saw children from Pine Ridge Public School and Pine Ridge Headstart, in Wounded Knee District the children were sampled from Manderson Day School and Manderson Headstart, and in White Clay District the children same from Loneman Day School and Oglala Headstart. Table 2 presents the age and six distribution for our sample, and Table 3 details what proportion of children at each age level came from each school sampled.

As a rough approximation, we note that for the reservation population as a whole, slightly more than 50% of the children from ages 0-14 years are male, and just under 50% of this age group is female. Thus, our sample is fairly representative of the total population, with respect to sex.

Table 2. Age and Sex Distribution of our Experimental Population

	Number	Age	Male %	Female %	Freq. Male	Freq. Female
	10	4-5	50	50	5	5
	10	5-6	40	60	4	6
	10	6-7	70	30	7	3
	10	7-8	30	70	3	7
	10	8-9	70	30	7	3
	10	9-10	60	40	6	4
	11	10-11	63	37	7	4
Totals	71		54	46	39	32

Table 3.   Distribution of Children Included in the Sample,
by Age and School

Age	OHS	MHS	PRHS	LDS	MDS	PRPS
4–5	5	5				
5–6	3	4	3			
6–7				1	1	8
7–8				1	6	3
8–9				8	1	1
9–10				10		
10–11				10	1	
Totals	8	9	3	30	9	12

Note: OHS, MHS, PRHS are Oglala, Manderson, and Pine Ridge Headstart,
respectively, LDS and MDS are Loneman and Manderson Day School, and
PRPS is Pine Ridge Public School.

Thus, roughly half (53%) of our population came from Oglala
Headstart and Loneman Day School, and about one-quarter each came from
Manderson and Pine Ridge.

Table 4 presents the distribution of our sample by age and
ethnic group, and presents comparable data for the reservation population at large.

With respect to degree of Indian blood too, our total sample
reflects very well the reservation population of 4- to 11-year-olds.

In our interest to incorporate the experimental findings and
data analysis into the larger social and cultural pictures of reservation life, we include the following descriptive statistics on
household language preference of family, and data on whether the
subjects home has water and electricity. Again, the results for our
experimental population are presented together with the parallel
statistics for the entire reservation population.

Table 5 presents the household language preferences for the
families of the children included in our sample, and for the general
population as well.

Table 5 shows us first that our sample population closely respects the total population in the languages it speaks at home. Thus,
we note that English as the preferred tongue is far more common in
Mixed Blood than in Full Blood homes, and while at least one-quarter
of the Full Blood population prefers to speak Lakota at home, a relatively much smaller percentage of Mixed Bloods share this preference.

Table 4. Distribution of Indian Ethnic Group by Age, for
Experimental Population and Reservation Population

Age	Experimental Sample		Total Population	
	% Mixed Blood	% Full Blood	% Mixed Blood	% Full Blood
4-5	66	37	59	41
5-9	77	23	58	42
10-11	37	63	54	46
Totals	55	45	57	43

Table 5. Household Language Preference by Ethnic Group

Language	Experimental Sample			General Population		
	% M.B	% F.B	% Ind	% M.B	% F.B	% Ind
English only or Mostly English	81	7	47	72	13	41
English and Lakota equally	11	65	36	25	62	44
Lakota only or Mostly Lakota	8	28	17	3	25	15

Table 6. Electricity in Household by Ethnic Group

Electricity	Experimental Sample			Total Population		
	% M.B	% F.B	% Ind	% M.B	% F.B	% Ind
Yes	75	21	51	81	40	60
No	25	79	49	19	60	40

Table 6 presents the percentages of children in our sample who have electricity in their homes, and the parallel statistics for homes in general.

Thus, although our sample population reflects accurately the trends seen in the general population, it tends to over-represent those homes in which electricity is not available. In both cases we see that the availability of electricity in the home is far more likely in a Mixed Blood than in a Full Blood home.

Table 7. Water in Household by Ethnic Group

Water	Experimental Sample			Total Population		
	% M.B	% F.B	% Ind	% M.B	% F.B	% Ind
Yes	72	10	45	61	19	40
No	28	90	55	39	81	60

Table 7 presents the distribution amongst Indian groups of the availability of an inside source of water in the home.

Once again we see that our sample tends to reflect accurately the availability of water in the home for the general population. The experimental population, however, does tend to increase the difference already found on this variable, between ethnic groups. We should explicitly point out that fully 90% of our Full Blood sample has no inside-the-house source of water.

In short, our normal sample of 71 children, seems representative of the general reservation with respect to sex, ethnic group, home language preference, and the ready availability of water and electricity in the home. In connection with Table 5, it was sometimes necessary to administer our tests in Lakota, through a translator. It will later become clear that the children with whom this was necessary suffered no resultant handicap.

V

Results

INTRODUCTION

Our results and analysis is going to be preceded by some practical psychological consideration including some aspects concerning the method that has been used here in order to experiment. Let us remember, that almost from its inception, a constant and growing concern of psychology has been the understanding and evaluation of how we think. These processes of thought, broadly termed cognition, have been chiefly evaluated in one way, namely, by measuring their static outcome. In other words, it has been assumed that thinking is a process by which we gained knowledge; thus, to evaluate one's ability to think we may simply assess how much knowledge he has gained. From this background has come most of our current measures of intelligence.

However, one may reasonably ask if this mode of assessment is truly fair. In fact, it seems intuitively clear, and has been empirically shown, that tests which seek to measure the outcomes of thinking - the knowledge gained - are necessarily bound to the social milieu and particular culture in which, and for which, they have been designed.

To make this clearer, let us step back for a moment and briefly outline the means by which these standard IQ tests give us information about an individual's "intelligence." If we may take the most widely used individual IQ test as an example, we see that it is composed of several sub-tests each of which is supposed to tap a relatively different function of thinking. Again, these sub-tests are based on the assumption that if we tap what is learned - either

51

facts or their application — we may get a practical statement of how well one can learn his IQ. But how are these IQ's gotten?

When these tests are first composed they are given to large numbers of people and the results obtained are treated statistically to tell us how the "average" person, at any age, would do. Also through statistics, we may obtain a way of seeing how any score compares to this average score. Thus, if the "average" person is defined as one getting an IQ of 100, we may make precise statements about how much better or worse someone else in a comparable group does, by relating his score to the "average."

Here is the critical point. What does "comparable group" mean? Our standard IQ tests tend to consider all people in the same age group as comparable. But if these tests are culturally based, as indeed they are, may we compare people of similar age, but of different cultures or subcultures, with fairness? When the "average person" with whom comparisons are made, has grown up and developed in one cultural setting, and when the very test we use reflects this cultural bias, does it make any sense to attempt to attach a number from this test to a person in a very different group who has developed through a different set of experiences? Clearly it does not. This is so because the number is quite meaningless — it can only tell us about the common learning outcomes of both groups and not the individuality or uniqueness of the new cultural group. Typically what is discovered is that groups unlike those for which the standard tests are based, do not perform as well on such tests — the people look "less intelligent." This, in fact, has been found at Pine Ridge in previous testing. Thus, if we are cautious we can say that people in ghetto communities, people of different cultures, people, for example at Pine Ridge, do less well on these tests than do people in some other areas; if we are rash we may say these people are less intelligent. This though, is the outcome of a testing situation which is not culturally fair.

A second point is even more fundamental. Let us even imagine that the standard testing procedures were perfectly fair for use at Pine Ridge. Then what? Although we might gain information on how well people perform here relative to people in general — that is, obtain an IQ score — we would know very little about what underlies their ability to learn. What we would obtain is a static outcome — a number — but at best only little information about the way in which people think. Why is this important? Most simply, if we are to be of any aid in betting the education and perhaps the total environment setting, we must first understand individual and group strengths and weakness in cognition, and the subtleties of the very processes of thought. For only if we first understand the very underlying mechanisms of learning and thinking can we hope to be of aid. Then too, we may ask, what is so sacrosanct about pinning numbers on people anyway?

If it is true that we may often be mislead in our evaluation of intelligence, school performance, etc., simply because we have not carefully questioned the appropriateness of the tests we use, what can we do? Fortunately, the highly significant work of Piaget over the last 40 years, seems to offer a more positive approach. Piaget has offered a formal description of the development of thinking, and gives us a system which deals essentially with the processes by which we gain knowledge, and not merely with the contextual knowledge that we have gained.

Thus, the methodology of this research contrasts very much with the standard testing approach, because it is essentially exploratory rather than static or statuatory - IQ tests do not seem to offer the essential flexibility implied or demanded by work with different ethnic groups, personalities, or social environments. In contrast, Piaget's method, the one used here, is a developmental one and has been called the Clinical Exploratory Method.

THE CLINICAL METHOD: A METHOD OF EXPLORATION

Essential to this technique is its flexibility, which consists in adapting the interview continually to the reactions of the child trying to follow his thinking process at each moment. The child must express himself spontaneously, either verbally or through his behavior, and the experimenter then seeks to enter into the child's own views. It is, then, central that the experimenter does not seek to distort the child's views by imposing his own order, but rather, that he follows the child - his words, his actions, his intent. Thus, the technique and the particular experiments applied give only the general framework, and the detail of the experiment depends very much upon the reactions of the child. This too contrasts, we believe basically, with standard IQ procedures, for they tend to be rather inflexible and represent a rigid approach to a dynamic problem.

Thus, in this method, each item is first presented in a uniform way, with no intervention from the experimenter the focus is on the spontaneous thoughts of the child. One must first be certain that the child understands the question - either verbally or behaviorally - and it is only then that the clinical method is applied to see what level of thinking the child may reach. Therefore, the results we obtain indicate the level on which the child is situated.

We may emphasize that in the use of the Clinical Method:

1.   The presentation of the experiment gives an opportunity to motivate the child favorably, to put him in contact and to develop rapport with the examiner. For example, we might introduce the material with a story or have the child make up a story. This can be used to learn the child's language, so that the experimenter can follow suit.

2.   In varying the factors implied in the experiment (this is not usually possible in the standard approach), one can often obtain very good information about the value of the results obtained. For example, if we are uncertain of whether a child has offered a conceptual or perceptual solution to a problem, we may vary the perceptual factors further in our clinical exploration, and note the results.

3.   By varying the way or the order in which questions are asked we may be sure of whether the child has understood what he is asked. Thus, we may tell whether a child really understands, or is merely repeating some part of the question as his answer. If it becomes clear that a child does not understand the task at hand, then that experiment should not be applied, for an initial understanding of the problem is a pre-requisite of participating in the experiment.

4.   With certain children, certain parts of the experiment can be avoided when one has no question about the validity of the answers obtained.

5.   Justifications: Each time the child gives an answer, either verbally or through behavior, one must ask for a justification, "Why?" "How do you know?" "What would you do to show it's correct?" etc. The justification, of course, is central because it tells us much about the processes involved in problem solving and the stage of thinking that the child has attained. Let us emphasize that we have had success in obtaining non-verbal justification from non-talkative children. It is important though not to interrupt the child, and to obtain a spontaneous result rather than a provoked response.

6.   As a further means of establishing the validity of an obtained result, we employ the method known as Contra-Proof. This technique consists in a counter-suggestion given by the experimenter. We might say, for example, "But, you know, another child said just the opposite, . . . Was he wrong, are you wrong?" In this situation it becomes clearer how strongly the child maintains the conviction of his solution. The function of the contra-proof then, is to aid in the differentiation of borderline cases, between the operatory (logically organized) and non-operatory levels of functioning. Thus, it is used when there is question about the fidelity of the child's response.

7.   The protocols contain both a precise recording of the conversation between experimenter and child, and a precise description of the movements, constructions, explanations, and in general, everything the child did.

APPROACH TO THE ANALYSIS

We can distinguish at least two basic processes underlying the development of both logical and infralogical operations. The logical processes deal with classification and relations of order with whole objects whose position in space is of no importance. Thus, the logical processes are discontinued and from them derive some important concepts such as number. The infralogical processes on the other hand, involve concepts of space, time, and speed and thus deal with continuous properties whose position in space is important; from the infralogical processes grow, for example, concepts such as measure. An operational child is characterized by the fact that he is going to master basic logical invariances in logical processes as well as infralogical ones. These logical invariances have been investigated with basic concepts such as conservation. In particular, the operational period of thinking is characterized by the fact that the child not only possesses conservation but also reversibility, that is the possibility of concrete operation related to an active manipulation of objects. In short, the operation is the results of a process of differentiation coming from certain physical and logical mathematical experiences.

To assess the existence of an operation, there are some arguments which we have been interested in, in our experiments which will demonstrate that the child possesses conservation. We may distinguish three kinds of justifications. One is an argument of identity, in which the child bases his belief in conservation upon the premise that since nothing has changed, the quantity is maintained. The second argument, is an argument of reversibility. Here the child will imply that if we returned to the initial stage we will see that some logical invariances have been preserved, e.g. "You could put it back the way it was and you will see that it is the same." The third argument, called compensation, deals with the fact that the child is able to use the combine different parameters in the situation in order to justify his belief in conservation. For example he will describe that one parameter has moved one way, but another has moved the other way, therefore, the quantity remains the same.

We have used in our experiment three basic cognitive realms: conservation, spatial relations and elementary logic. One of the problems in making a study of cognitive development is to be able to assess the potentialities rather than the lacks in each individual. Thus, for this reason we have insisted upon making a broad cognitive analysis with three basic logical realms rather than confining ourselves one limited concept. Thus, until the child can remove himself from the concrete perceptual attributes of the problem he cannot offer an abstract point of view. Moreover, the child must do it consistently in many different contents; concrete operational thinking is not the ability to provide an operational behavior in one particular experiment but consistently in many various contents. Concrete operational thinking is a structure of thinking, and as we have insisted earlier, an operation is never isolated but is part of a whole structure. Thus, our concern in making a broad analysis of the cognitive development among our children. Moreover, if we consider the major acquisitions of the concrete operational level of thinking we observe that reversibility and conservation are its primary developments. Therefore, in each of our three realms: conservation, space, and elementary logic, we have been concerned about the mastery and the operation of reversibility.

Our procedure in the analysis of the results is related to our concern of evaluating these two aspects of cognitive development. In each experiment, the first part is devoted to a qualitative analysis of the succession of stages and for each experiment we will take examples of typical behaviors related to each particular stage. This will determine whether the succession of stages has been respected in our experimental population. A second aspect of our analysis is deductive in the sense that will provide some comparisons in terms of norms between Geneva and Pine Ridge. However, we wish to insist that this quantitative comparison remain simply suggestive since our population is limited in terms of the number of subjects although not in terms of the number of experiments each subject has taken. Earlier we stressed the fact that a broad picture of the cognitive development in qualitative rather than inquantitative terms is the goal of this research.

Finally, our analysis will be devoted first to each particular experiment and will deal later with a general appraisal of cognitive development. In terms of the statistics used, we have sometimes dealt with a Guttmann Analysis. This type of analysis, which deals with the elaboration of scalogram, is extremely fruitful method of assessing the concept and the continuity of stages. The application of Guttmann Analysis to Piaget stage sequences have been done in some other works. Pell [32a] has summarized several investigations of this type in the areas of space, logical judgment and moral judgment. Mannix is cited by Hunzer [32b] and Wohlwill [32c] had each done scalogram analysis in the area of numbers. The scalogram procedure is used to find out the extent to which a set of responses interpreted by Piaget as representing different stages of development within a given content area, do in fact form a genuine developmental progression. Responses on level B presuppose responses on genetically more immature level A; responses on level C presuppose responses on A and B and so on. We have been able to proceed in such a way with some experiments and we are going to discuss the results obtained through this scalogram procedure. In particular, Mannix and Wohlwill found an orderly progression in the mastery of various Piaget related number tasks by scalogram analysis. In short, our analysis is primarily qualitative in terms of the elaboration of the succession of stages, although it is quantitative when dealing with the comparison between Pine Ridge and Geneva norms and with the use of a Guttmann Analysis.

LOGICAL REALM CONSERVATION: CONSERVATION OF MATTER

This experiment which is based on one of the early works of Piaget [33] has been conducted according to the following technique:

Material. Two plastic balls of clay.

Presentation. The child is made to observe the equality of both quantities. He is asked to make two balls, A-1 and A-2. And then is asked "Do we have the same amount to eat, or do I have more or do you have more?" Following his answer, he is asked, "How do you know?" If the child disagrees that the balls are equal, E has him add or take away clay so that both have the same amount to eat. That is, have the child adjust the balls so that he sees them equal whether this is objectively true or not.

Part 1

The experimenter transforms one of the clay balls into a sausage shape and asks "Do we still have the same amount to eat or do I have more or do you have more?" He then asks why. Following this the experimenter returns the sausage shape to its own original form and asks the same question as before, namely, now do we have the same amount to eat, do I have more, do you have more, and why.

Part 2

The experimenter takes ball A and makes it into a pie shape, then ask the same question as above and why. He then returns the pie shape back to its initial form and again repeats the question and asks for the justification.

Part 3

The experimenter transforms one of the balls into several little pieces that are spread or deployed in space. Then he asks "If I would eat all those and you would eat all that do we still have the same amount to eat do you have more do I have more?" "Why?" Then the experimenter puts all the little pieces back together and now asks the same question as above. Again comparing the two clay balls.

In other words we have three situations in these experiments which are schematized by the following diagram:

Part I	A $\longrightarrow$ B	
Part II	A $\longrightarrow$ C	
Part III	A $\longrightarrow$ D	

Piaget has described three stages in the acquisition of the conservation of matter.

Stage 1: no conservation; the quantity of matter changes according to its transformations. In most cases the sausage (B) contains more matter (most frequent answer) but sometimes it is the ball which contains more. The main aspect of this stage is the fact that the child does not believe that conservation of matter is preserved during a transformation. This is usually characteristic behavior of children between 4 and 5.

Stage 2: is characterized by an empirically founded on and off sort of conservation. The child is transitional in the sense that he affirms conservation for some transformations but denies it for others; usually he does not resist the contra-suggestion. In other words, at this stage the child alternatively affirms and negates the conservation. This is the usual behavior of children between 6 and 8 years.

Stage 3: The child is no longer mislead by the perceptual appearance of the situation; conservation is present as a logical necessity. The operatory child understands logical invariances and supports his belief with one of three arguments. Because these justifications are the same for all four conservation experiments, we will summarize them now. The first argument that the child may use is an argument of identity. This is both the most primitive and most frequent justification for conservation. For instance, he points, "The shape is different but it is always the same matter". The second argument, that of compensation, may proceed somewhat like this: "It is longer, but it is also thinner, therefore, the matter is the same." Compensation is usually characterized by some coordination between the parameters; involved in verbal terms by the use of the comparative. In the third justification, the argument of reversibility we find for example that the child will tell us, "If you put this back into a ball you will see that we have the same." It should be noted that one of these justifications must be used by the child in order to assess the presence of conservation although all three need not be displayed in a particular experiment. One of them is sufficient in one experiment to determine the presence of conservation.

Although no statistics are readily available in the book of Piaget, our results show that we may qualitatively distinguish the three stages as described by Piaget in our experiment.

The results given in percentages, demonstrate that we are able to follow the same succession of stages in Pine Ridge as has been observed in Geneva. For instance at age 4, we find that 100% of the children fail to present any form of conservation either at stage 2 or 3. At age 5, we see that already one third of the subjects are at

Table 1.   Results of Conservation of Matter

Σ = 69	4	5	6	7	8	9	10
Acquired (stage 3)	0	0	30	40	60	60	64
Intermediate (stage 2)	0	34	30	10	30	10	18
Failure (stage 1)	100	66	40	50	10	30	18

stage 2. Whereas 66% of the subjects are still at stage 1 that is, clearly pre-operational.

We observe a quasi-equal repartition of the subjects in all three stages at age 6 where already 30% of the children have acquired conservation, 30% are at stage 2, and 40% are still at level 1. At age 7, we find a very slight decrease at stage 2 which moves toward an increased in percentage at stage 3 (40% at level 3). The great leap, however, is situated between 7 and 8 where we observe that almost two thirds of the subjects possess conservation; this situation is maintained for the subsequent ages, where we find respectively 60%, 60% and 64% of operatory behavior.

It is interesting to note that one third of the subjects are still at stage 2 at 8, while only 10% fail conservation whereas almost one third of the subjects of 9 years fail conservation. Our limited number of subjects cautions against a premature interpretation of these findings. Primarily, what should be noted about these results is that conservation seems to be acquired around age 7 and 8, since we observe that consistently from 8 to 10 years the majority of subjects master it. 69 children have passed this experiment.

The comparison with Geneva is also interesting. If we group the children according to the way that it has been done in Geneva, we find a comparison of norms between Oglala and Geneva children.

Table 2.   B. Comparison with Geneva

Σ = 69	5		6		7		8		9	
	O	G	O	G	O	G	O	G	O	G
Acquired (stage 3)	0	16	30	16	40	32	60	72	62	84
Intermediate (stage 2)	17	0	30	16	10	4	30	4	14	4
Failure (stage 1)	83	84	40	68	50	64	10	24	24	12

O = Oglala   G = Geneva

As stated above, our norms are only suggestive since our number of subjects is limited. In particular, we observe that at age 5 in Oglala 83% of the children fail to present conservation whereas in Geneva 84% fail; that is, almost the identical of failures are present in both samples. Another interesting point, also not significant, is the fact that 17% of the children in Oglala are at the intermediary stage (level 2) whereas none of the children in Geneva are there. At 6, the comparison reveals 68% failure in Geneva and 40% failure with the Oglalas. On the other hand, we observe that at 6, 30% of the children already possess conservation among the Oglala while only 16% of the children possess it among Geneva children. Again, we want to insist that these differences are not to be taken literally. The comparisons remain valid at 7 where we find 40% Oglala children and 32% of the Geneva children possess conservation with 50% of the children still failing in conservation among the Oglala Sioux and 64% among the Geneva children. At 8, however, there are only 10% of the children who still fail conservation among the Oglala, and 24% among the Geneva children; whereas 60% of the Oglala children and 72% of the Geneva children succeed. At 9, the situation is again comparable. Here we find 80% success in Geneva and 62% of success among the Oglala children. Generally speaking, the progression of stages is comparable with that of Geneva. In short, with the Pine Ridge sample, conservation of matter presents a succession of stages parallel to the succession observed with Geneva children.

Let us take some examples which will make our point clear. These examples are taken directly from the protocols; we will illustrate each stage by two or three examples relevant to the characteristic patterns of behavior presented within each stage.

Subject 504/14 points to the length of the sausage in order to demonstrate that the experimenter has more to eat. He tells us, ("You have more because yours is like that.") When the ball of clay is transformed into pie, he says, ("I have more because it's bigger.") When the ball of clay is transformed into pieces, he says, ("You have more because your have those pieces.")

Another characteristic example is subject 603/23, who tells us that the sausage is bigger than the ball. When asked how she knows this she tells us, ("Because I'm smart - I know which one is long because I have eyes - because it's real long.") Again, when one of the balls is flattened into the shape of a pie, she says, ("You more - when it gets spread out it's the mostest.")

Clearly, these subjects are typically pre-operational; they do not believe in conservation and their reasons lie in typical pre-operational justifications.

Subject 505/15 is typically on level 2 in the sense that even if she tells us at the first transformation that we have the same amount to eat, ("Because they look the same.") When she comes to the pieces, she tells us, ("You have more now because you broke yours in pieces.") If asked if the cutting into pieces makes it more, she says, ("Yes, you have more.") Further she does not resist the contra-suggestion.

Subject 605/25 alternatively affirms and negates conservation and therefore is also at level 2. For example, if asked, after having told us that we have the same amount to eat when it was a pie, to respond to the contra-suggestion she tells us that the other boy is right, the ball is more. "Ball is more?" ("Yes.") "How do you know?" ("Because it's bigger.")

Typically operational, that is to say at level 3, is subject 704/34. He believes that we always have the same amount to eat if the ball is transformed into a very long snake. He tells us, ("It's the same, if I crush it up like that, it will be the same around.") Or in the case of the pie, he tells us, ("It's the same because this is flat and that's round, but if I crush this up it be the same round.") Or in the case of the pie, the pieces, he tells us, ("You could put them all back and they would look the same.") We observe that this subject alternatively uses three types of justification for conservation reversibility in order to support his belief.

Typical also of operational behavior is subject 709/39. In the case of the snake he tells us, ("We have the same because when this one is rolled up they're both the same.") He uses here an argument of identity whereas in the case of the pie he tells us, ("We both have the same because when this one was a round ball they were the same and you just flattened it.") This child is able to make use of two arguments, identity and reversibility, in the same experiment, in order to assess his belief in conservation.

In short, these examples are typical of pre-operational, transitional, and operational behavior.

CONSERVATION OF LIQUID

These experiments which have been described in Piaget's book, "The Child's Conception of Number" [33], is characterized by the following experimental procedure.

Material. Two identical glasses called A-1 and A-2 - A=reference glasses. One glass higher and thinner than A, called B. One glass shorter and wider than A, called C. Four little glasses having identical form, each to contain one quarter the volume of A, these called D-1, 2, 3, 4. Three little glasses of identical form, each to contain one third the volume of A, called E-1, 2, 3. Two bottles of colored water of different colors.

Presentation. The experimenter takes A-1 and A-2 and say "You see these two glasses, they are equal." E takes one of the bottles and pours water into A-1. The child takes the other bottle and himself pours the same amount of water into A-2. (Child should do it for himself but the experimenter can do it for him.) In this critical first step the child is to recognize the identity or equality of quantity in A-1 and A-2. Thus, the experimenter says, "If you drink from A-1 and A-2, will we have drunk the same amount, will I have drunk more, or will you have drunk more?"

Part 1

The experimenter pours water from A into B and then asks, "Have we now the same amount to drink or do you have more or do I have more?" and then asks why. Once a justification is given, the water is poured back from B into A and then the same question is asked as in the presentation. "Do we now have the same amount to drink, do you have more, do I have more?"

If there is confusion about levels, the child is permitted to make the correction that he feels has to be done to make the quantities equal.

Part 2

The water is poured from A into C and the same procedure as in the first part is carried through.

Part 3

The water is poured from A into D so that the four levels in D are equal. The procedure of the first two parts, is followed but E insists that the comparison now deals with all four little glasses as opposed to A. Thus, the experimenter might ask, "If I were to drink all this water in all these glasses and you were to drink the water in this glass (pointing to A) would be have the same amount to drink, would you have more, would I have more?" Once again, after the child gives his answer and justification, the water is poured back from D into A and once again the child is asked, "Do we now have the same amount to drink, do you have more, do I have more?" and is asked why.

Part 4

The water is now from A into E, such that the three levels in each of E are visibly different; once again the experimenter asks, "If I were to drink all of this water (pointing to the three levels in E) and you were to drink this water (pointing to A) would we have the same amount to drink, would I have more, would you have more?"

This experiment can be schematized in the following way:

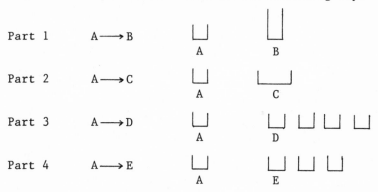

Part 1	A ⟶ B
Part 2	A ⟶ C
Part 3	A ⟶ D
Part 4	A ⟶ E

Again, three stages have been described for the acquisition of the conservation of liquid. Stage 1 is characterized by no conservation. Children of stage 1 have no difficulty in recognizing the equality of liquid in the identical glasses, but when the contents of one of the glasses is poured into another glass of a different shape, the quantities are no longer judged as equal. Either glass B contains more because the level is higher (most frequent answer), or glass A contains less because it is less wide. The reason involved can vary (differences of level, width, number of glasses), according to the situation, from one subject to another, and from one moment to the next. The main point is that the change perceived is seen as giving birth to a modification of the total quantity of liquid.

Stage 2, is characterized by a conflict between conservation and nonconservation, with perception and logic alternatively getting the upper hand. It is a transitional stage with intermediary answers and vacillation of thinking. Children of this stage are capable of affirming conservation but they do not affirm it as a logical necessity. In other words, they alternatively affirm and negate the conservation. Moreover, they usually do not resist the contrasuggestion.

Subjects of stage 3 conceive conservation as a logical necessity basing it primarily on a coordination of the different parameters, such as height and width. At this stage the child immediately conceives conservation independently of the number or nature of the

pourings done in front of his eyes. As justification for conservation he may use either one, two, or all three of the operatory
arguments for conservation; identity, reversibility and compensation.

An analysis of the results shows us that the 67 subjects who
have taken part in these experiments behave in the following manners.

Table 3. Results of Conservation of Liquid

Σ = 67	4	5	6	7	8	9	10
Success (stage 3)	0	0	10	30	30	70	64
Intermediate (stage 2)	0	0	50	30	50	20	36
Failure (stage 1)	100	100	40	40	20	10	0

Some interesting results appear when we consider this table.
First, at age 4 to 5, we observe 100% failure, whereas at age 6, we
observe that 50% of the children are at stage 2. Furthermore,
already 10% of the children in the conservation of liquid, presenting
therefore stage 3 behavior. At 7 and 8, we observe that one third of
the subjects at these ages have already attained stage 3 for the
conservation of liquid, whereas, at 7 years old, 30% of the subjects
are at level 2, and 40% are in complete failure. 50% of the subjects
are at level 2 at age 8, and only 20% still present a picture of
complete failure. The big jump, then, is situated between 8 and 9,
for where 70% of the subjects are at stage 3 at 9, only 30% are
operatory among 8-year-olds. At ten, 64% of the subjects completely
succeed, and 36% are in stage 2.

In short, this picture reveals again a complete succession of
the stages. They are qualitatively the same as were observed in
Geneva: at 4 and 5 no conservation, at 6, 7, and 8 approximately half
and half, with half of the subjects being at level 2, and at 9 and 10
the majority being at stage 3. When we proceed to a comparison with
Geneva, we observe the results shown in Table 4 (we should note again
that the comparison is done with the same age grouping as in Geneva).

The comparison with Geneva is interesting in the sense that we
observe complete failure at age 4-5 for both Geneva and Oglala children, with 100% with the Oglala Sioux vs 85% with Geneva children.
Moreover, at age 6, we find the identical percentages of failure at
Geneva and Pine Ridge, 40% in both cases; almost the same percent is
at an intermediary level, stage 2: 50% for Oglala Sioux, 42% for

Table 4. B. Ages Grouped as in Geneva

	4-5		6		7		8-10	
	O	G	O	G	O	G	O	G
Success (stage 3)	0	4	10	18	30	74	55	87
Intermediate (stage 2)	0	11	50	42	30	22	35	11
Failure (stage 1)	100	85	40	40	40	4	10	2

O = Oglala   G = Geneva

Geneva children, and almost the same percent is at level 3, that is, a level of success. Somehow the picture is a little bit different relative to subjects of age 7. There for the Oglala we observe that approximately one third of the subjects are at level 3, one third at stage 2, and 40% at stage 1, whereas in Geneva, there are 74% of the children who succeed at age 7, with the conservation of liquid. But again, these differences should not be emphasized since, because of the limited number of subjects, they can be only suggestive. The changes occur between 7 and 8 for the Oglala, where we observe that the majority of the Pine Ridge children are at level 3. In Geneva, however, this jump comes between 6 and 7 where it is maintained throughout the remaining age groups. The point is, that although there seems to be a one year time delay in the acquisition of conservation of liquid for Oglala children, the most important finding is that the succession of stages is completely respected in the Pine Ridge sample children. In order to illustrate further our point let us take some examples of the different stages, from Oglala children protocols:

Subject 603/23 is typically pre-operational. She tells us that we have more to drink in B because it was poured into a different glass. ("My glass is little and yours is big and it fills it up.") In C, she tells us that she has more coffee in C because ("Yours is little and mine is big, and you pour it in, it's little.")

On another hand, subject 608/28 believes that we have more to drink in glass B, ("You have more because it is very tall.") When it is poured into the little glasses, E1, 2, 3 he says to us, ("You have more to drink because you have three cups.")

On the other hand, typical of intermediary behavior at level 2 is subject 602/22 who in situation B points to the level and says, ("You have more. It's in a bigger cup.")

He resists the contra-suggestion and says, ("I am right,
more here.") He changes direction however, for situation E
and says that we have the same to drink. In other words,
he is typically on an intermediary level.

On another hand, subject 709/39 is typically at level 3,
that is, an operational level. For situation B he says,
("Still same even if you pour it here it stays the same
because this is skinnier and this is fatter.") In C, he
tells us again that they are the same. ("The first time
they were both the same level. If they were the same in
there and you poured it all in there (C) it stays the
same.")

Subject 902/54 is also on level 3. He tells us that in
situation B there is the same amount. ("Mine's fat and
yours is skinny, but mine is short and yours is tall.") In
other words, he clearly makes use of an argument of compensation. He continues to use this argument with the next
situation (C) where he tells us with a laugh. ("That's the
same, this is round and fat and yours is tall and fat.")
This child is typically operational. Again, what we
observe is that the reaction of the children here is
comparable in every way with the reaction of Geneva
children.

CONSERVATION OF WEIGHT

Conservation of weight has been described in the same book as
conservation of matter, by Jean Piaget and Barbel Inhelder [34].
The technique of this experiment is the following:

Material. Same as in conservation of matter, plus a Roman scale.

Presentation. The child is asked about the scale, what it does, how
it works. The experimenter explains its working to him if necessary.
Then he asks, "If I would put this one here and this one here, would
they weigh the same, would they balance, and why?" (E does not actually put the clay on the scale unless it becomes necessary to prove
to the child that they do weigh the same.)

Part 1

The experimenter transforms one of the clay balls into a sausage
shape and asks, "If I would put this sausage shape on the scale and
this ball onto the scale, would they still weigh the same, or would I
have more, or would you have more?" and "Why?" Then the experimenter
puts it again to the original ball shape and repeats the question and
again asks for a justification.

Part 2

Now the experimenter transforms one of the clay balls into a pie shape and again asks the same question and asks for a justification. Then he transforms the pie back to its original shape and again asks the same question and asks for a justification.

Part 3

The experimenter cuts up one of the balls into many small pieces spread out in space and again asks the same questions above. Then he transforms it back to its original shape and asks the same questions as above.

In other words, the technique is very similar to the one followed in the conservation of matter except that a real balance scale is presented to the child. Again, three stages have been described; they are almost identical to those described in the conservation of matter. In other words, a stage 1 of no conservation, where the quantity of weight changes according to perceptual transformations of the material, a stage 2 of transitional behavior, where the child alternatively affirms and negates the conservation, and a stage 3 where conservation is conceived as a logical necessity. It has been described and proven again and again that conservation of weight is acquired later than the conservations of matter by Geneva children. We have found again not only the same succession of stages as in Geneva, but also the same time delay, at least in qualitative terms. In other words, the overwhelming majority of children who succeed the conservation of number are not assured to master conservation of weight. If we consider the results obtained by our subjects who have passed this experiment, we observe the following distribution:

Table 5.   Results for Conservation of Weight

Σ = 30	7-8	9	10
Acquired (stage 3)	53	85	70
Intermediate (stage 2)	16	0	20
Failure (stage 1)	31	15	10

This table shows us that around 7-8, there are 53% of the children who are at level 3 and almost one third who are at level 1, that is a level of failure; 16% of the children are intermediary. Clearly, it is around 9 that weight is acquired. 85% of the children present conservation of weight at 9 whereas only 15% fail and none are transitional. At 10, we still find that a majority of the children possess conservation of weight 70%, while 20% are at level 2, and 10%

are still at level 1. When we make a comparison with Geneva, and group the subjects the same way that Geneva has done, we observe that:

Table 6. B. Comparison with Geneva – Conservation of Weight

	8		9		10	
	O	G	O	G	O	G
Acquired (stage 3)	53	52	85	72	70	76
Intermediate (stage 2)	16	8	0	12	20	8
Failure (stage 1)	31	40	15	16	10	16

O = Oglala   G = Geneva

At 8, 53% of the subjects among the Oglala children possess conservation of weight as compared with 52% who possess it in Geneva. 85% at 9, possess conservation among Oglala, and 72% among Geneva children, and at 10, 70% of the children possess it among Oglala and 76% among Geneva children. Clearly, the picture is comparable in every sense between the Geneva and Pine Ridge samples.

For example, subject 804/44, who is clearly at level 2 for the conservation of matter is at level 1 for the conservation of weight. In this experiment he tells us, pointing to the snake, ("This one is more, because this is heavy and this is light.") "How do you know?" ("Because this is into a ball and it's heavy.") Pointing to the pie he tells us, ("This one will be more heavy because this is real flat and heavy.") In other words, this child is clearly at level 1, for the conservation of weight.

Another child, 108/69, is at level 3 for the conservation of matter, and at level 2 for the conservation of weight. In particular, he tells us, ("The ball would weigh more – it's bigger.") After the contra-suggestion, he agrees that they weigh the same, but given another situation with the snake, he tells us, that the ball would weigh more because it's bigger. Finally, he tells us again that they are the same because the shape doesn't really matter. In other words, this child is clearly at level 2, for the conservation of weight.

Some other children, 110/71, for example, are clearly operational for both conservation of matter and conservation of weight. This child tells us that both balls weigh the same. For the snake, she says, ("This one weighs the same as that one...these two are the same amount.") This subject clearly manifests operative functioning.

We observe then, that the same time delay between conservation of weight and conservation of matter is displayed in both samples. More importantly, however, we find that in conservation of weight the Oglala children follow the same succession of stages as is observed in Geneva; this remains our main point.

CONSERVATION OF LENGTH

Conservation of length has been described in the "Child's Conception of Geometry," by Jean Piaget, Barbel Inhelder, and Alina Szeminska [35]. The technique used in the experiment is the following:

Material.   Two sticks of equal length (A-1 and A-2)
One stick shorter than A-1 and A-2 called B
One stick shorter than B called C
2 little horses

Presentation.   The experimenter asks the child to choose two sticks of the same length. (For little children (ages five to six) the investigator asks why he hadn't chosen one of the other sticks). The experimenter now puts A-1 and A-2 in a horizontal and parallel position about one or two inches apart. They must be directly contiguous; that is, without one extremity passing over another. He then asks, "Are they still the same length?" and "Why?" if the child does not understand the concept of length, he says, "If this horse would go along this pathway, and if this horse would go along this pathway, would one walk more than the other, would both walk the same and why?" This first part of the presentation is performed in order to establish in the child's mind, and in the experimenter's mind, the child's understanding that the two sticks are of equal length.

Part 1

The experimenter says, "Watch carefully what I do." He then takes A-1 and displaces it by an inch or two to the right and then asks, "Are these two sticks still of equal length, is one longer than the other and how do you know?" If the child doesn't understand, the experimenter may make use of the horses as above. Then the sticks are returned to their initial position and the questions are repeated.

Part 2

The investigator proceeds as in Part 1, this time displacing A-1 an inch or two to the left.

Part 3

The procedure is the same as above, but this time the experimenter simultaneously moves A-1 to the right and A-2 to the left,

saying, "Look carefully at what I am doing." Then he proceeds with
the questions as above. Then he moves the sticks an inch or two
towards the left, again asking the same questions as above.

Conservation of length has been described by Piaget, Inhelder,
and Szeminska, in "The Child's Conception of Geometry." The concept
of length-conservation is usually acquired around the age of nine.
As in the other tasks dealing with conservation, length-conservation
calls for the establishment and understanding of an equivalence. The
child is asked to determine the equivalence and to display his understanding of logical invariancies after transformations of the initial
configuration. This requires a coordination of the parameters involved, namely the constancy of length and the realization of the
compensation factor involved in the displacement.

Stage 1: Stage 1 is characterized by the child of about five or
six who has little idea of conservation. Children at this stage do
not recognize the equality of length except when the sticks are put
in direct optical correspondence. It is a stage of global comparison.
The child is incapable of anticipating the quantitative meaning of
the transformation. As soon as the optical correspondence is broken,
the notion of the equality of length disappears. Three types of
errors account for the failure to recognize the maintenance of length
equality.

Type I: The child maintains that stick A which overpasses stick
B, at that point, is longer. This most frequent response shows
the focus of the child to be on the movement of the displacement
of the sticks. This justification for the lack of equality in
length allows for no compensation for the equal but overlapping
sticks.

Type II: The child makes a judgment of length inequality based
upon the inequality of "space." The child will point to one end
of the stick and reports that the lengths are unequal because
the sticks do not take up the same amount of space.

Type III: There is a mixture of Type I and Type II errors,
errors of other kinds, or a reasoning where it is difficult to
decide if it is Type I or Type II.

Stage 2: Behavior characterizing this stage can be described as
vacillating. The child is transitional in that there is a conflict
between the concept of conservation and no conservation of length.
Perception, or misperception, and logic alternately obtain the upper
hand. The concept of conservation of length is not stable, the child
sometimes affirming and at other times negating it. This behavior
appears around the ages of seven or eight.

Stage 3: This stage is characterized by the conception of conservation as a logical necessity. At this moment the child of around nine years bases his conclusion through the coordination of the parameters involved. One of the three operatory arguments, identity, compensation, or reversibility, is used to justify his belief in the logical invariances.

The results were as follows:

Table 8.   B. Ages Grouped as in Geneva

N = 66	4-5		6		7		8		9	
	O	G	O	G	O	G	O	G	O	G
Success	6	8	50	4	45	20	40	68	80	96
Failure	94	92	50	96	55	80	60	32	20	4

O = Oglala   G = Geneva

Failure seems to be characteristic for 4- to 5-year-old children; 94% of the children fail within Pine Ridge group and 92% among Geneva sample. At 6, we observe the interesting fact that almost 50% of the children succeed among Oglala children whereas there are still 90% of the children who manifest complete failure among Geneva children. At 7, we find that 80% of the children in Geneva fail and only 55% among Oglala children fail. At 8, the picture is a little different, with 68% of the Geneva children succeeding while 40% of Oglala children do so. At 9, however 80% of the children succeed among the Oglala children and 96% succeed among the Geneva children. In other words, we can say that the major jump from a failure to success is situated around 8-9; this is true for Oglala as well as Geneva children. Briefly, among the 66 subjects who participated in this experiment the results found were very comparable to Geneva norms, implying that the succession of stages is again respected. Nevertheless we again insist that because of the limited number of subjects, our comparison is primarily qualitative.

We observe here, that a majority of the subjects between 4 and 5 manifest Type 1 errors, whereas the distribution of the errors between Type 1 and Type 2, tends to be equal later. For example at 8, we find approximately one third of the subjects making an error of Type 1, and another third of the subjects committing a Type 2 error. In short, it is interesting that of the 55% of the subjects who make errors for the total distribution of our sample, 32% manifest Type 1 errors, and 22% manifest Type 2, where Type 3 is almost unrepresented. That is, both errors are almost equally frequent; the

error of basing the judgment wholly on the movement of the displacement of the sticks and that of basing the judgment of equality upon
the amount of empty space at one end.

If we consider the distribution of type of errors, we obtain the
following table:

Table 9.   A. Distribution of Types of Errors

	4	5	6	7	8	9	10	Total Errors
Type 1	66	60	30	22	30	22	10	32
Type 2	22	30	20	34	30	8	0	22
Type 3	12	0	0	0	0	0	0	1
Total	100	90	50	56	60	30	10	55

A comparison with Geneva according to the type of error, is
again fruitful.

Type 1 error: The displacement in space is not compensated.
Type 2 error: Centration in the inequality of spaces.
Type 3 error: Others.

Table 10.   B. Comparison with Geneva of Type of Error

	4-5		6		7		8		9-10		Total Errors	
	O	G	O	G	O	G	O	G	O	G	O	G
Type 1	63	64	30	84	22	63	30	24	16	4	32	47
Type 2	26	16	20	0	34	14	30	0	4	0	22	6
Type 3	5	12	0	12	0	3	0	8	0	0	1	7
Total	94	92	50	96	56	80	60	32	20	4	55	60

Here again, when we group the subjects in the same way that it
has been done in Geneva, we observe that Type 3 errors are as in-
frequent in Geneva as they are among Oglala children. Errors of Type
1 are almost as frequent among Oglala as they are among Geneva children, while Type 2 errors are considerably more frequent among Oglala
as compared to Geneva children (32% vs 6% respectively). At age

4-5, we find 63% of the children making an error of Type 1 among the Oglala children, and 64% among Geneva children. Interestingly, there are at 6, 84% of Geneva children will still manifest an error of Type 1 while only 30% of the Pine Ridge children will present it. Again the repartition between Type 1 and Type 2 errors is almost equal among Oglala children of age 7, (22% vs 34%) whereas, we find the overwhelming majority of the children making an error of Type 1 (63% vs 14%) among Geneva children. But given the fact that we find the same types of errors is in itself suggestive. Again it is helpful to take some examples to further illustrate our point.

Child 606/26, for example is clearly at level 1 in the conservation of length. With the first displacements she tells us, ("This one's short, and this one's long because you move that one up, this one is more long") she clearly is at level 1.

The same is true for child 607/27, who after the first displacement says, ("It's bigger – this one is higher, and this one is lower"), as she points to the moved stick. As at the second transformation she tells us, ("You pushed this one down – it's shorter").

On another hand, subject 504/14 is clearly at level 2. After the contra-suggestion he points to the displaced sticks and tells us, ("It's longer because it's way up here") ("So this is longer?" "They're even). ("Well show me – how is it?" "Even"). Faced again with the contra-suggestion he says, ("They are not even, this one is longer"). This child demonstrates vacillation of thinking and is clearly at level 2.

The same is true for the subject 706/36, in the conservation of length. After the first displacement she tells us; first pointing to the displaced sticks, ("No this one is longer, because it moved"). With the second confirmation she tells us with hesitation ("This is longer, we moved it"). but at the contra-suggestion she says, ("He was right, no one is longer"). She typically presents a picture of transitional behavior.

Some children however, are clearly at level 3, such as child 900/52, who tells us no matter how the sticks are placed ("They're still the same") or subject 901/53, who tells us after the first confirmation, ("Put it together and it's the same"), and she does so spontaneously. In other words she clearly makes use of reversibility.

In short, conservation of length again presents a parallel between Geneva and Oglala children relative to the succession of stages. The interesting fact can be noted that since conservation of length seems to be a perceptual task in theory at least we should see this conservation acquired since it is perceptually strongly imbedded in the situation. In other words, it is very easy to observe that by direct observation the two sticks are equal, and yet children manifest difficulty in determining it as long as they are not operational in their thinking. The reason is that conservation is not perceptual and consists really of an abstraction. In other words, the abstraction of an operation which seems to be perceptually easy is not at all easy for a child who does not think in operational terms. We have observed this situation among both Oglala and Geneva children. We will return to this point when we talk more precisely about learning experiments and pedagogical implication.

ONE-TO-ONE CORRESPONDENCE

The one-to-one correspondence has been described by Piaget in his book "The Child's Conception of Number" [33]. The experiment here is concerned with conservation, but we would like to point out that there are two properties which are stressed in this experiment.

The first is the establishment of equivalence, the ability to determine the same number of objects as the examiner has, the second is to make a judgment about conservation and to justify it. If conservation of length deals with the conception of measure, the one-to-one correspondence deals with the concept of number, the mastery of each requires operational arguments such as reversibility and the construction of logical invariances.

The description of the technique is the following:

Material. 9 horses, 12 of another animal (for example, lions).

Presentation. (a) The experimenter asks the child how many horses there are. (b) He then orders the horses in front of the child, such that they are side by side, with 4cm intervals between horses. The lions are put in disorder in front of the child.

Experiment

(1) The investigator says to the child, "Take enough lions for these horses. Put one lion in front of each horse. Put them together so that we have only one lion for each horse."

(2) The experimenter leaves the horses as they are, but extends the lions in space. Whereas in Part 1 the rows should be arranged like this:

```
......... Horses
......... Lions
```

For this part the configuration is as follows:

```
......... Horses
 . . . . . . . . . Lions
```

He then asks: "Is there still 1 horse for each lion?" "Are there more horses, more lions?" "How do you know?"

(3) The investigator asks the child: "If we put them as before, would we now have one horse for each lion?" Then he rearranges them as in Part 1.

(4) He leaves the lions, and extends the horses in space as in Part 2. Then he asks the questions as above.

At this point, we would like to emphasize that our technique consists of a slightly modified version of the technique usually presented in the book. Instead of eggs and egg cups which are un-known here among Oglala children, we have used horses and lions but otherwise have followed the same procedure as that required for Geneva children. Since the procedure is the same we are entitled to make some comparison between Geneva and Oglala, but let us state first the description of the stages as have been found in Geneva.

In stage 1, the child has neither equivalence nor conservation. In other words, he tries to make the spatial arrangement come out the same and does not use a one-to-one correspondence method. This stage is characterized by an incapacity to predict the quantity of the element. This stage is usually characteristic of children around 3 to 4.

In stage 2, the subject can establish equivalence but not con-servation. At this stage the child spontaneously makes use of the method of one-to-one correspondence. He understands how to place an object opposite another one and knows its cardinal value without counting, but when the optical correspondence is destroyed by spread-ing out or closing up one of the rows the child gives up his earlier belief in cardinal equivalence. The longer row is thought to contain more objects by virtue of its length (more frequent answer) and sometimes the more compact one has more by virtue of its density (less frequent answer). In all cases, conservation disappears when the optical correspondence is destroyed in front of the child.

Stage 3, occurs around 6, 7 and 8, when the child establishes both equivalence and conservation indicating that the logical struc-ture of number has become more powerful than the perceptual im-pression of the space occupied. Conservation has become a logical necessity which is explained either by identity ("You did not take anything away, all you did was move the objects") or reversibility, ("You could put them back the way they were before"). The equality is maintained regardless of the perceptual aspects. The results in terms of stages are the following:

Table 11. A. Results in Terms of Stages

	4	5	6-7
Stage 1	40	0	0
Stage 2	50	40	46
Stage 3	10	60	54

We observe again a succession of stages. At 4 years, 40% of the children are at stage 1; 50% at stage 2; and 10% at stage 3. At 5, we observe that no children are still on stage 1, whereas 40% are at stage 2 and 60% are at stage 3. Around 6 and 7 the percentage of children at stage 3 is 54%, clearly the majority of the children pass at stage 3 between 4 and 5.

A comparison with Geneva can be made and is shown in Table 12.

Table 12. Comparison with Geneva

	4		5		6-7	
	O	G	O	G	O	G
Success	10	8	60	50	54	75
Failure	90	92	40	50	46	25

O = Oglala   G = Geneva

We observe if we group the subjects in the same way as has been in Geneva, that 90% of the Oglala children fail around 4, as compared with 92% of the children in Geneva. The overwhelming majority of the children fail the one-to-one correspondence at age 4. At 5, however, the picture is half and half, 50% of the subjects succeed in Geneva and 60% in Oglala. At 6-7, 54% of Oglala children succeed whereas 75% of the subjects in Geneva succeed. Again, we want to stress that the comparison is suggestive rather than quantitative. Nevertheless, the point remains that the Oglala children do behave in the same progressive manner as do Geneva children. Let us take some examples of the different stages.

Subject 402/2 is at stage 1, for the one-to-one correspondence. In particular, she lays down horses in rows but
does not place them in one-to-one correspondence. She uses
all of the elephants and in quite a natural way she tells
us that there are more horses and more elephants. She
tries to make the spatial frontiers come out even and does
not use the method of one-to-one correspondence.

Some children like 501/11 are already at stage 2. For her,
as soon as the optical correspondence is broken, the number
of horses is greater. She tells us when the horses are
extended that there are more horses. The same remains true
for subject 503/13, who is also at stage 2. He believes
that there are more elephants because they are spread
further apart, and yet he is able to establish an equivalence.

Subject 505/15 however, is already at stage 3. This
subject tells us, ("No more horses than elephants because
they are all spread out"). When the elephants are spread
out, she says, ("The same but spread out. They are spread
out but it is the same").

Subject 602/22, is also at stage 3. She tells us when the
horses are extended that it is the same. "How do you
know?" ("I put them in front and they were the same"). In
other words, we observe here both the equivalence and the
conservation of number which is justified with an argument
of reversibility.

Discussion of the Results in Conservation

Our five experiments dealing with conservation: matter, liquid,
length, weight, and the one-to-one correspondence, consistently provide us with an image in which the succession of stages in cognitive
development is respected. In each conservation study, an acquisition
is required. That is, the child has to discover that certain features
of an object remain invariant in the wake of substantive changes in
other attributes.

The observation of the succession of stages is central in assessing the logic of cognitive development. If we try to summarize
the principle findings in Piaget's studies, we observe that each type
of quantity concept, like matter and weight, shows about the same
developmental trend, namely, stage 1, no conservation; stage 2,
transitional behavior; and stage 3, conservation conceived as a
logical necessity. The other major finding is that despite the
apparent similarity among tasks in the conservation of matter and
weight, we do observe that they are not achieved at the same time.

If for Piaget's subjects conservation of matter seems to become
common at age 8, for weight we observe a 2 year time delay. This is
also observed with our Pine Ridge sample. As Flavell states [36].

"The interpretation of these findings is complex and
detailed, but the key elements appear to be the following.
There are probably two developing schemas which together
contribute to the acquisition of matter conservation, ie.
conservation of the global "amount of stuff" in the piece
of clay. There is first the general capacity to multiply
relations...[but] The second schema, closely related to the
first, is called atomism...Again, the belief in conservation becomes more probable if the child can conceive of
the clay as a whole composed of tiny parts or units which
simply change their location vis-a-vis one another when the
whole undergoes a transformation of shape. Conservation of
matter is here the expression of the fact that the total
sum of these parts remains the same, whatever their spatial
distribution."[36](p.300)

And yet one should be careful about many points which can be
made concerning the acquisition of conservatory behavior. One of the
important features of the development of operational thinking consists in the understanding of two very distinct elements in reality:
space and transformations. This distinction is very important especially for conservation. As we have insisted above, we can distinguish between two fundamental aspects in thinking; the figurative
aspect, which essentially consists of a description of the state, and
the operatory aspect which permits the understanding of the transformation, that is, the pathway from one state to another. Before
having structured logical operations the child reasons only on the
basis of the state and in an essentially figurative way. For a child
to present no conservation or even to be at stage 2, where he vacil-
lates, indicates a conflict between the perceptual appearance of the
reality, namely the figurative aspect, and the operatory aspect, that
is, the logical invariances involved. In order to understand the way
that reality behaves in transformations, the child must understand
the reversible operation, and this is what he will use when he is at
an operational level of thinking. The point we want to make is that
a transformation from one state to another does not transform all the
features of the situation at the same time; it transforms only certain aspects of it while certain others remain constant. We can also
observe this in every mathematical or physical transformation. When
a child has achieved operational behavior he begins to display a
comprehension of reality. The figurative aspect of thinking is under
the control of the transformation; therefore one of the essential
acts of intelligence consists in building and understanding the
transformation of reality. In other words, if the figurative aspect
of thinking is necessary because we have to have a knowledge of the
state in order to understand the transformation, it is the trans-

formation which explains the state and not the state that explains
the transformation. Briefly the figurative aspect of thinking is
subordinated to the actions and operation. That is, the figurative
aspect play a role only as a necessary auxillary.

A final point that we would like to note is the fact that the
transformation has to be effected in front of the children. A recent
article by Bever and Mehler [37] deals with the cognitive capacity of
very young children. These authors took children between the ages of
2.6 and 3.2 and tried to get them to correctly discriminate the
relative number of objects into tows. They observed that the discriminative ability of the younger children showed that "the logical
capacity for cognitive operation exists earlier than previously
acknowledged." The point is, that in none of their experiments were
the transformations done directly in front of the children. The
configurations dealing with the one-to-one correspondence were presented statically to the child rather than in a dynamic manner. As
long as the transformational aspects of the situation are not done in
front of the child, then the situation remains a figurative one which
does not require operational functioning in order to be discrimi-
nated.

In our experiment we have strictly respected the Geneva procedure and discovered that we could superimpose the succession of
stages. In short, the five experiments dealing with the logical
realm of conservation display a picture of similarities of development between Geneva and Oglala.

LOGICAL REALM: SPATIAL RELATIONSHIPS

Geometrical Drawings

Geometrical drawings have been described in the book written by
Jean Piaget and Barbel Inhelder, "The Child's Conception of Space"
[38]. In this experiment the child is asked to copy a series of 21
geometrical drawings which are intended to tap the child's sense of
topological and Euclidean relations. It has been found particularly
discriminative between 3-, 4-, and 5-year-olds. The description of the
technique is the following:

Technique. We begin by asking each child to draw a man from memory,
both to put the child at his ease and to give ourselves some idea of
his natural drawing ability. Next we ask him to copy, either wholly
or partly, the following series of models. It will be noticed that
some of the models emphasize topological relationships while others
are simple Euclidean shapes. A third group combine both types of
relationship (total or partial interlacing of Euclidean figures,
etc.)

(1) A large irregular shape 4-5cm long with a small circle 2-3mm in diameter outside but close to the boundary. (2) The same with small circle inside and close to the boundary. (3) The same, with the circle astride the boundary. (4) A large circle. (5) A square. (6) An equilateral triangle. (7) An ellipse. (8) A rectangle twice as long as wide. (9) Two circles 1cm apart. (10) Two identical circles in contact. (11) Two intersecting circles. (12) A circle circumscribing an equilateral triangle whose points touch the circumference. (13) A circle containing an equilateral triangle, apex at the center and base resting on the circumference. (14) A circle 4cm in diameter with a small equilateral triangle of 1.5cm side placed at the center. (15) An equilateral triangle of 4.5cm side containing a circle tangential to the three sides. (16) An identical triangle with a circle 4cm in diameter intersecting its sides to form three equal segmental arcs. (17) A square having a single diagonal. (18) A rhombus of 4cm side. (19) A similar rhombus bisected by a horizontal diagonal forming two equilateral triangles. (20) A vertical horizontal cross. (21) An oblique cross. We have reproduced the figures in Figure 1.

Let us begin first with a description of the stages as given by Piaget. At stage 0 we observe simple, rhythmic movements. At stage 1, we observe the first differentiation of the forms dominated pri-

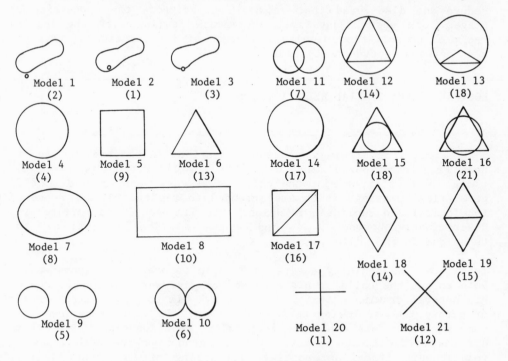

Fig. 1.   Description of the geometrical figures.
Numbers used for our sample are in parentheses.

marily by scribble. A first stage, level 1a consists of modification
of the scribble under the influence of the models. We observe dif-
ferentiations according to the concepts of open and closed forms, but
only certain aspects of the model are respected. At stage 1b, we
observe drawings where the topological relations are clearly indicated but the Euclidean relations are not mastered. We also observe
the beginning of closed curves and therefore closed circles. Stage
2 consists of the beginning of differentiation of Euclidean forms.
At stage 2a, we observe no differentiation between rectilinear forms,
squares and triangles. The drawing length and angles are marked
without taking into account their numbers. Most of the time the
rectangle is right. The figures dealing with a relationship of both
total or partial interlacing of Euclidean figures are usually not
succeeded. The simple rhombus is not succeeded either. In other
words, at stage 2a the enclosed figures are reproduced without sufficient analysis of their contact points. Stage 2b is characterized
by a success in the rhombus and a progressive composition of the
enclosed figures, with the exception of the most integrated, interlacing one. Stage 3 is characterized by a complete success in all
figures including those which represent an integration of both types
of relationships, topological and Euclidean ones. We have been able
to perform a Guttmann analysis with our results, so that we will
analyze later the respective difficulties of each figure as presented
by the Oglala children. In short, we have attempted a type of standardization of the results, in order to determine the progressive
difficulties among the figures and to assess again our point about
the succession of stages.

If we consider the results in terms of stages we observe that
the children follow the stages described in Geneva.

Table 13. Development of the Geometrical
Drawings

	4	5	4	5
1a	20	0	50	0
1b	30	0		
2a	40	15	50	40
2b	10	25		
3	0	60	0	60

The majority of the subjects are divided between stage 1 and
stage 2 at the age 4. 50% of the children are at stage 1, with 20%
at stage 1a and 30% at stage 1b. 50% of the children of age 4 are at
stage 2, with 40% in stage 2a and only 10% in stage 2b. At 5, the
picture is considerably different in the sense that no children are

at stage 1a or 1b, 40% of the children are still at stage 2, and 60% of the children have attained complete mastery of the 21 geometical drawings dealing with complex Euclidean and topological relations. This fact is interesting. Clearly between 4 and 5 we have a jump; from 50% of the children who are at level 2 at 4, we observe that 60% of the children are at stage 3, at 5. At five 15% are still at stage 2a, 25% are at stage 2b, and no children are at stage 1a or 1b. Our analysis at this point shows a regular evolution as described by Piaget. Although we did not have any three year olds we observe that no 4-year-old presented a 3-year-old behavior, i.e., no 4-year-old children were at stage 0. When we compare the numbers of success within figures among Oglala and Geneva children, we observe that the circle is succeeded between 4 and 5 by 100% of the children among Oglala children and by 84% among Geneva children. At 5, both populations succeed in the circle. The main points of the comparison is given by the following table:

Table 14. Geometrical Drawings.
Figures classified according to their increasing difficulty

			4-5		5-6	
			0	G	0	G
1a	(4)	IV	100	84	100	100
2a	(5)	IX	100	16	100	50
3a	(11)	XX	100	94	100	100
4a	(1)	II	90	84	100	100
5a	(2)	I	90	74	100	100
6a	(3)	III	80	87	100	100
7a	(6)	X	80	55	100	93
8a	(7)	XI	80	68	100	93
9a	(8)	VII	80	87	100	100
10a	(9)	V	50	52	100	83
11a	(10)	VIII	50	65	100	100
12a	(12)	XXI	40	36	100	77
13a	(15)	XIX	34	23	91	70
14a	(16)	XVII	20	24	91	70
15a	(13)	VI	20	36	91	93
16a	(14)	XVII	12	13	75	70
17a	(17)	XIV	10	42	75	100
18a	(20)	XVI	10	10	58	37
19a	(18)	XIII	0	17	58	73
20a	(19)	XII	0	13	50	63
21a	(21)	XV	0	20	50	53
		%	50	48	88	82

1a = Order of increasing difficulties.
(4) = Numbering of our sample.
I   = Numbering of Piaget's description.

Following a Guttmann analysis the figures have been classified according to their increasing difficulty. But before dealing with it, it is interesting to note the close similarities of age of success among Oglala and Geneva children from 4 to 5. We observe that 50% of the Oglala children succeed vs 48% for Geneva, whereas between 5 and 6 the percent success 88% vs 82% between Oglala and Geneva children between 5 to 6. This by itself would be sufficient to determine that spatio-temporal relationships develop among Oglala children in the same way as has been described in Geneva. But when we make use of Guttmann analysis we can demonstrate that the three stages are sequentially well represented.

First, the level of inconsistency of our scale is less than 5%. We observe .06% of inconsistency, that is, plus in the realm of the minus, and 1.4% of inconsistency for the number of minuses in the realm of the plus. Clearly the level of inconsistency is not significant. Moreover, we observe that the scale clearly distinguishes three stages.

Stage 1 indicates that all subjects who succeed in the ellipse will have succeeded all previous figures, whereas the subject who succeeds the ellipse is not necessarily going to succeed the square. This clearly implies that the pathway from topological to Euclidean relations indicates a clear stage.

Similarly, stage 2 is characterized by the subject who succeeds the square as well as all previous figures, which are representative of topological relations. That is, the subject at stage 2 manifests mastery of Euclidean and topological relations although he lacks a mastery of their integration.

There is also a clear break between success at Euclidean relations and success in figures which represent an integration of topological and Euclidean relations together. Clearly, a child who succeeds the last figure will have succeeded all the previous ones. This fact is important because it means again that mastery of Euclidean and topological relations together is indicative of stage 3 functioning.

In short, we observe the successive mastery of first topological relations (stage 1), then Euclidean relations (stage 2), and finally of their integration (stage 3).

In other words, the Guttmann analysis provides us not only with a sequence of stages which correspond to the sequences described by Piaget but also with an organization of the figures according to a level of increasing difficulty. For example among our 22 subjects, 22 succeed with the simple circle as well as the two circles and the cross, and 20 succeed in all the topological relations; whereas 17 succeed until the square and only 6 are successful up to the most

Table 15

Geometrical drawings.

Guttman's analysis

Figures organized by order of increasing difficulty.

Subjects classified only by success and failure.-

Obs. no.		4	5	11	1	2	3	6	7	8	9	10	12	15/16	13	14	17	20	18	19	21	Succes	Failure	
		1a	2a	3a	4a	5a	6a	7a	8a	9a	10a	11a	12a	13a	14a	15a	16a	17a	18a	19a	20a	21a		
1.L	402/2	+	+	+	o	o	o	o	o	o	o	o	o	o	o	o	o	o	o	o	o	o	3	18	
2.L	403/3	+	+	+	+	+	o	o	o	o	o	o	o	o	o	o	o	o	o	o	o	o	5	16	
3.L	401/1	+	+	+	+	+	+	+	+	+	o	o	o	o	o	o	o	o	o	o	o	o	9	12	
4.L	405/5	+	+	+	+	+	+	+	+	+	o	o	o	o	o	o	o	o	o	o	o	o	9	12	
5.L	408/8	+	+	+	+	+	+	+	+	+	o	o	o	o	o	o	o	o	o	o	o	o	9	12	
6.L	404/4	+	+	+	+	+	+	+	+	+	+	+	o	o	o	o	o	o	o	o	o	o	11	10	
7.L	501/11	+	+	+	+	+	+	+	+	+	+	+	+	o	o	o	o	o	o	o	o	o	12	9	N
8.L	409/9	+	+	+	+	+	+	+	+	+	+	+	+	N	o	o	N	o	o	o	o	o	12	7	+2
9.L	406/6	+	+	+	+	+	+	+	+	+	+	+	+	+	+	o	o	o	o	o	o	o	14	7	
10.L	504/14	+	+	+	+	+	+	+	+	+	+	+	+	+	+	+	o	o	o	o	o	o	15	6	
11.L	407/7	+	+	+	+	+	+	+	+	+	+	+	+	+	+	o	o	+	+	o	o	o	16	5	
12.L	410/10	+	+	+	+	+	+	+	+	+	+	+	+	+	+	+	+	o	o	o	o	o	16	5	
13.L	507/17	+	+	+	+	+	+	+	+	+	+	+	+	+	+	+	+	o	o	o	o	o	16	5	
14.L	505/15	+	+	+	+	+	+	+	+	+	+	+	+	+	+	+	+	+	o	o	o	o	17	4	
15.L	506/16	+	+	+	+	+	+	+	+	+	+	+	+	+	+	+	+	+	o	o	o	o	17	4	
16.L	508/18	+	+	+	+	+	+	+	+	+	+	+	+	+	+	+	+	+	+	+	+	o	20	1	
17.L	503/13	+	+	+	+	+	+	+	+	+	+	+	+	+	+	+	o	+	+	+	o	+	19	2	
18.L	509/19	+	+	+	+	+	+	+	+	+	+	+	+	+	+	+	+	+	+	+	+	+	21	0	
19.L	510/20	+	+	+	+	+	+	+	+	+	+	+	+	+	+	+	+	+	+	+	+	+	21	0	
20.L	601/21	+	+	+	+	+	+	+	+	+	+	+	+	+	+	+	+	+	+	+	+	+	21	0	
21.L	606/26	+	+	+	+	+	+	+	+	+	+	+	+	+	+	+	+	+	+	+	+	+	21	0	
22.L	502/12	+	+	+	+	+	+	+	+	+	+	+	+	+	+	+	+	+	+	+	+	+	21	0	
	+	22	22	22	21	21	20	20	20	20	17	17	16	14	14	14	10	10	8	7	6	6	325	137	462
	o	0	0	0	1	1	2	2	2	2	5	5	6	8	8	10	12	12	14	15	16	16	% 70.3	29.7	
						I								II						III					

Level of inconsistency {No. of inconsistencies + = 2 0.6; − = 2 1.4} < 5%

	I	II	III
+	188	110	27
o	10	66	61
	198	176	88
+	94%	62%	30%
o	6	38	70%

complicated figure, drawing 21. Thus, in Table 14, we have classified our figures according to their increasing difficulty. We note
that the cross is overwhelmingly succeeded by our subjects and since
a comparable analysis does not exist with the Geneva sample, we will
say that the main trends hold. The circle is succeeded, and there is
only one discrepancy between Oglala and Geneva children which concerns success for the two circles which the majority (100%) of 4 year
old Oglala children succeeds as compared with only 16% of the Geneva
sample. The reason is most likely the fact that our circles were
further apart than those shown to Geneva children, and therefore
could have been perceived as two distinct circles, thereby rendering
distinct the topological relation. The Guttmann analysis was used
essentially to assess the normality of the development and the succession of stages. We have been able to show that clearly we observe
a transition between a mastery of the topological relations and that
of Euclidean relations followed by a situation where we find success
in both Euclidean and topological relations together.

We would point out, that the geometrical drawing constitutes a
very good experiment for children who do not talk. For instance one
could argue that the investigator tends to be suggestive, thereby
distorting the results; in order to confront the problem of suggestibility, we have taken two precautions. The first is that we used an
interpreter with all subjects whose primary language was Lakota, but
much more to the point of suggestibility, a problem which arises in
those experiments which give flexibility to the clinical method, is
the fact that the geometrical drawings can be taken without a word
coming from the experimenter. This is the reason why we provided a
Guttmann analysis in assessing the sequence of stages since clearly
suggestibility cannot interfere either in the copying of the geometrical drawings or in this method of interpreting the results.

In short, it is to answer both questions; the question of
suggestibility and that of the sequence of stages that we have constructed a scalogram analysis. It is reassuring to observe that
given this strict method of analyzing the development of stages we
found them to be essentially the same as was observed in Geneva.
Furthermore, that we were able to show the same changes in understanding spatial relations at the same age is also encouraging and
tends to demonstrate impressively that the cognitive development of
spatial relationships proceeds in the same manner among the Oglalas
as it does among Geneva children.

ROTATION OF LANDSCAPE, OR COORDINATION OF PERSPECTIVES

This experiment, which has been discussed in the book of Piaget
and Inhelder "The Child's Conception of Space" [38], is concerned
with the discrimination and coordination of spatial perspectives, as
well as with an appraisal of the child's egocentrical point of view

dealing with his ability to put perspectives into relations. We should mention that we have modified this test so that it could be used as a learning experiment although not a learning experiment in the usual sense. What we have tried to do is to see the ways in which a child could use information provided to him. In particular we have insisted upon a checking of each particular position by the child. In general, the way that learning experiments are done consists of presenting the child with a certain number of perceptual features which will enhance his ability to construct conservation. In our case what we have provided the child with is essentially only a correction through a checking of the position by the child himself. We were interested in discovering if the child had no ability to learn a local ability or could be taught more than one position at a time. In this sense our experiment also deals with the ability of the child to generalize information. What we will see later is that the child who is clearly pre-operational is not able to display a learning strategy other than a local one. This leads to the idea that there exists a relationship between his stage of cognitive development and his ability to integrate information but we will come to this point later.

Relative to the comparison with Geneva, our results are based essentially upon the spontaneous achievements of the child. Again we want to insist that our comparison with Geneva remains only suggestive, given the difference of content and the difference of technique. This experiment is new in the sense that we have provided a learning modality to the child. The description of the technique is the following:

Material. 2 identical boards, 2 lions, horses, houses, trees, 1 screen.

Presentation. The experimenter and child sit side by side, and the experimenter constructs a landscape using the house, horse, and tree on his board. He then asks the child to name elements in landscape, and then to construct one that is exactly the same.

P1 With experimenter and child sitting at right angles to each other, the experimenter places his lion at one side of his board and the child's lion at the corresponding side of his board. The child is now told to construct a landscape as the experimenter's lion sees it. Note that for success in this experiment, the child must remove himself (in thought) from where he is sitting and anticipate how the landscape appears from the experimenter's point of reference.

P2 Same as in (1) except that experimenter's board is now rotated an additional 90°.

P3 Same as above, with 90° more rotation.

P4   Same as above, with 90° more rotation. Thus, in P1 through P4,
the landscape is moving but the observer remains stationary.

Part II(b)   In this series of rotations, the landscape remains fixed,
but the lion, or reference point waries through four steps.

Part III(c)   Lion is placed at a corner of the board, and the point
of view is from the diagonal.

Three stages have been described for the acquisition and coordination of perspective and spatial relationships. Stage 1, is characterized by an incapacity to understand the question itself.

Stage 2 is generally characterized by a egocentric point of
view. We observe a complete lack of differentiation between the
subjects point of view and the point of view of the other observer.
In stage 2a, we observe representation essentially centered on one
point of view. The subjects are incapable of understanding that
different observers are going to have different perspectives. In
other words, we do not observe any spontaneous deductions of the
necessary transformations implied by the change of position of the
observer. We observe no spontaneous inversion of the relations left,
right, forward, backward, and relative position. In stage 2b, we
observe attempts at spontaneous differentiation but essentially the
child falls back into an egocentrical construction. In other words,
we have here trials of dissociation of different points of view but a
failure because of inadequately relating the perspectives. The
subject begins to anticipate the relativity of certain spatial relations according to different points of view but manifests no general change. In other words, the relativity is dependent upon the
position of the observer in some elements of the configuration.

Stage 3 is characterized by differentiation and increasing
coordination of perspectives; in other words a relativity of point of
view. In stage 3a, we observe differentiation of certain relations
according to changes of position of the observer but no whole spontaneous coordination. The subject in other words possesses a true
but incomplete relativity. We have no spontaneous comple domination
of simple spatial relations. In stage 3b, we have a spontaneous
understanding of simple perspectives and a true and complete relativity of point of view in which any position of the observer corresponds to a system of relation. In other words, any point of view is
related to the relative position of the observer.

Our results clearly indicated that we had to differentiate
furthermore between two types of spatial relations; two levels of
differentiation on simple and complex transformations. We will come
to this point later. This experiment has provided us with an understanding of the nature of spatial relations. For example, we will
see that such distinctions are important in order to assess which

type of difficulties can be overcome by certain children at a given age, according to their level of development. In order to introduce a problem let us first do a comparison between Geneva and Oglala children.

Table 15b. Logical Realm: Space. Rotation of Landscape: Perspectives

		7		8		9		10	
		O	G	O	G	O	G	O	G
	Success	13	13	37	12	23	13	45	66
PART I	2 errors	37	26	50	44	55	71	38	31
	+3 errors	50	51	13	35	22	16	17	3
	Success	25	19	37	33	45	52	54	75
PART II	Failure	75	81	63	67	55	48	46	25
TOTAL	All items included								
	Success	19	0	37	13	32	26	37	43
	Failure	81	100	63	87	68	74	63	57

It should be noted that for the Oglala children we have taken into consideration only the errors of inversion. Each different position was considered as one set of measures; we have taken into account the initial performances without any interference from the experimenter.

In Part 1, the board is rotated from 90° and so on, when we count errors as done in Geneva we observe 7-year-old children only are 13% successful both in Pine Ridge and in Geneva. With two errors we find that 37% of the children behave this way for Oglala as compared with 26% of Geneva children. More than three errors is characteristic of respectively 50% and 51% of the Oglala and Geneva 7-year-olds. At 8, the situation is somewhat favorable for success among the Oglalas but not very much. The same situation remains at 9, but at 10, we observe that 66% of the Geneva children demonstrate a successful Part 1, while only 45% of the Oglala children do.

In terms of Part 2, that if we count only the success and failure, we observe that the acquisition of spatial relationships is late for Oglala children. Only 54% of the subjects at 10 succeed, whereas we find 75% of the subjects succeeding in Geneva. However, it is interesting to note that in both cases, Part 1 and Part 2, Pine Ridge children are somewhat ahead of their Geneva peers until the age of 10.

All items including Part 1 and Part 2, provide us with a global picture of Oglala and Geneva norms. We would like to insist that for

10-year-old children neither a majority of the Oglala nor Geneva children succeed (37% vs 43% respectively). Let us emphasize again that the performance of the Oglala children and the Geneva children are quite comparable in the sense that both samples behave in almost the same way.

We have provided an analysis in terms of stages and by ages. But first we must indicate the two types of confirmation that we have been dealing with in our equipment.

The first type of confirmation occurs when only the object had to be moved and not the basic reference level, i.e., the cardboard itself. It was our purpose to have chosen a rectangular cardboard because its rotation is asymetrical. In this sense P1 and P3 are simple transformations. The second type of confirmation, i.e., P2 and P4 involve the rotation of both the basic reference cardboard and the objects on the cardboard themselves.

Let us remember that an experiment as simple as copying the horizontality of the water level is succeeded very late; for instance we observe that only 52% of the Geneva subjects at age 10 are able to succeed in copying the horizontality of the level of liquid.

The problem is identical to our experiments because it means that the subject must be able to decenter in a simple way positions such as P1 and P3 in which essentially the inversion of objects left, right, backward, and forward has to be taken into consideration; or his decentering may involve a double change such as in situations P2 and P4. It is interesting to note, that the development of spatial relationship can be distinguished in our experiments according to these two levels of transformation. As a matter of fact, we were even able to distinguish the stages in terms of what we would call local errors and errors of inversion. For instance, at level 2a the child does not provide any systematic change of a relative point of view which means that he is going to manifest errors of inversion. This remains true for all subjects who are at level 2a or level 2b, whereas at level 3, we will observe what we have called local error, an error involving the position of one object but which indicates that a general change is involved.

Thus, we can state that positions such as P2 and P4 involve formal operations since what the child has to do is an operation on operations. Better said, this type of configuration is transitional between the operational level of thinking and the formal level of thinking. And it could explain in a way, why only 52% of the children succeed, and so few subjects succeed at 10, all items included. We should remember, that 57% of the children still fail at 10 among Geneva children and 63% among Oglala. Let us observe the result in terms of stages and ages for simple concrete transformations, namely, situations P1 and P3.

Table 16.   Experiment: Perspectives

| | Results in terms of stages and by ages 16A | | | | | | 16B | |
	1	2a	2b	3a	3b	1	2	3
P1 + P3	6	0	28	0	36	36	0	28	72
(simple concrete	7	0	0	0	30	70	0	0	100
transformations)	8	0	0	20	20	60	0	20	80
	9	0	0	11	23	66	0	11	89
	10	0	17	17	8	58	0	34	66
		9	10	23	58	0	18	82

If we would have restricted ourselves to simple concrete transformation, namely, transformation where the basic reference level has
not changed then we could conclude that already 72% of the children
6 years old are at stage 3. None of the children manifest stage 1;
therefore, all present a relative capacity to understand the problem
posed.

Concerning the repartition in terms of sub-stages (16A) we
observe that level 3a is represented among all the ages. 36% of the
children at 6; 30% at 7; 20% at 8; 23% at 9; and 8% at 10. 3A has a
tendency to decrease, whereas 3b tends to increase. We should note
that the real gap is situated between 6 and 7, where 36% of the 6-
year-old children are at level 3b; whereas 70% of the children are at
level 3b at 7. In other words, a minority is at level 3b at 6; and
an overall majority is at 3b at 7. In short, it is the analysis of
the sub-stage which reveals operational development, and we observe a
clear leap from 6 to 7. The level 2a and 2b are not well represented;
only 28% of the subjects are at this level at 6, while we observe a
slight decrease at 10 to 17%. Most of the children remain at level
3a or 3b.

Very different is the picture when we examine the results
obtained with complex transformations which deal with an understanding not only of the changing of objects but also of changes of
the basic reference level itself.

We observe that for complex transformations level 2a and level
2b is characteristic of the majority of the subjects at 6, with 70%
of the children being at level 2. We observe here a contrasting
picture between these results and the results previously obtained.
At 7 we have a division of 50% and 50% between stage 2 and 3; at 8,
70% of the children are still at level 2 and this proportion remains

Table 17. Results in Terms of Stages and by Ages

		17a					17b		
		1	2a	2b	3a	3b	1	2	3
P2 + P4	6	0	81	9	9	0	0	90	10
(Complex	7	0	20	30	40	10	0	50	50
transformations)	8	0	30	40	20	10	0	70	30
	9	0	22	55	0	23	0	77	23
	10	0	54	18	9	19	0	72	28
		42	30	15	13	0	71	29	

almost the same for 9 and 10 - 77% and 72%. Its unfortunate that we do not have any Geneva statistics concerning the development in terms of stages, but we can make some interesting hypotheses for instance, clearly the level of difficulty of P2 and P4 is of a different order of magnitude as compared with P1 and P3. We should note too that the majority of the children remain typically pre-operational when faced with complex transformations. If only 28% of the children are at level 3 at 10, for complex transformation we can infer that this part of the experiment clearly deals with operation on an operation, that is, with formal operations.

When we put the results of simple and complex transformations together (P1 and P2, with P3 and P4) the picture becomes similar to the results obtained in Geneva.

Table 18. Experiment: Perspectives
Both Transformations Together

	18a					18b		
	1	2a	2b	3a	3b	1	2	3
6	0	55	4	23	18	0	59	41
7	0	10	15	35	40	0	25	75
8	0	15	30	20	35	0	45	55
9	0	11	33	11	45	0	44	56
10	0	34	18	9	39	0	53	47
	25	20	19	36	0	45	55	

We observe here a mixed picture; 59% of the children are on level 2 at 6; whereas 75% of the children are at level 3 at 7; interestingly this percentage decreases with increasing age so that we find 55%, 56%, and 47% at stage 3 for the 8-, 9-, and 10-year-olds. In total 55% of the children will be at level 3 at 10, if we consider both transformations together. In short, at age 8, level 2 with both transformation together, is characteristic of 45% of the subjects, while level 3 is characteristic of 55% of the subjects. Interestingly enough, the same situation is true relative to a differentiation between simple and complex spatial transformations when we take into account the learning strategy adopted by the children.

In this analysis we have distinguished four different ways in which the child integrates information. (1) He presents no learning (N); (2) He presents local learning (L); that is to say, he is able to correct one position at a time but no more than one; (3) He is able to demonstrate the learning of more than one position at a time (M); that is, he is already integrating some spatial relations, and finally, (4) He needs no learning or is able to generalize brief learning to almost all positions (GNL).

Table 19 shows us that in regard to simple concrete transformations (P1P3) 28% of the 6-year-old children do not manifest any learning. 18% display local learning, and already 45% do not need any learning, or are able to demonstrate generalized learning. When we compare these results with the results in terms of stages for P1P3, what we observe is that exactly the same number of subjects who

Table 19.   Experiment: Perspectives
Logical Realm: Space

		N	L	M	GNL
Learning for P1 + P3	6	28	18	9	45
	7	0	0	20	80
	8	0	0	40	60
	9	0	0	33	67
	10	0	27	19	54
		5	10	24	61

N = No learning.
L = Local learning (one position at a time).
M = More than one position at a time.
GNL = Needs no learning or is able to transpose a
short learning almost all positions.

do not show any learning (28%) are at level 2a. It clearly indicates the relationship between the level of pre-operativity of the
subject and his potential to be able to demonstrate learning. At 7
and 8, we find that 100% of the subjects are at level 3 of whom 20%
display a learning of more than one position at a time and 80% do not
need any learning and are able to generalize completely. Note that
no subject of 7 displays no learning or local learning for simple
transformations. Again, a clear relationship between the modality of
learning and the level of pre-operativity is implicated. The comparison is maintained at the later ages, justifying our differentiation between simple concrete transformations and complex ones. In
order to elaborate this point, let us examine the learning strategy
for positions P2 and P4.

Table 20. Experiment: Perspectives
Learning for P2 + P4

	N	L	M	GNL
6	28	63	9	0
7	0	50	50	0
8	0	20	70	10
9	0	33	44	23
10	0	36	45	19
	5	41	43	11

This table is interesting in the sense that we observe at 6,
that 63% of the children display local learning, whereas generalized
learning or no learning needed is almost never represented. The most
the children can do is to achieve a learning of more than one position at a time. For example at 8, 70% of the children display more
than one position at a time, and at 9, 23% demonstrate generalized
learning. Again, we observe a jump between 6 and 7, 9% of the subjects display learning of more than one position at a time at 6, as
compared with 50% of the subjects at 7.

Again, it is interesting to relate the learning data to the
results obtained for complex transformations. What we observe then,
is that 90% of the subjects are at level 2 at 6. 90% of the subjects
is almost the number of subjects who do not display any learning or
who manifest local learning. Further, 50% of the children are at
level 2 at 7; while 60% of the 7-year-olds display only local learning. At 8, we find 70% of the children demonstrating a learning of
more than one position at a time and 70% of the children who are

still at level 2. In other words, we observe here a complete reliability between the modalities of learning and the cognitive level
displayed in positions P2 and P4. Clearly also, we can say that if a
child is unable to function an operative level of thinking he is not
likely to manifest learning which is better than his operative level
allows him. Furthermore, local learning does not constitute learning
in the true sense of the term since it does not enhance the result;
in this regard the comparison is most interesting.

Table 21.   Experiment: Perspectives
Learning for P2 + P4

	N	L	M	GNL
6	28	45	9	23
7	0	25	35	40
8	0	10	55	35
9	0	16	39	45
10	0	21	29	50
	5	26	33	36

Upon examining this table, we observe that if we take both
transformations at the same time, P1, P2, P3, and P4, there are only a
few ⌈ 6-year-old children who are able to demonstrate generalized
learning (23%) at 6 to 40% at 7. Clearly our experiment is transitional between concrete operational level of thinking and a formal
level of thinking. If we now provide a comparison between the learning modalities and the stages, and the positions distinguished we
obtain the following curves.

These curves are interesting in many respects. First if we
compare the level of development for P1, P3 and P2, P4, we observe
that children of all ages do better for P1, P3. There exists a
difference of difficulty between the two types of relations which is
attested to by the fact that generalized learning is not characteristic of complex transformation P2, P4. For instance the learning
abilities are very small at all ages in P2, P4. Not even one-third
of the subjects can benefit from generalized learning in order to
succeed for P2 and P4. What really has to be explained is the fact
that the 7-year-old children provide better results in P2, P4 than
children at later ages. It could too mean that what we observe is
that they do not benefit from a modality of learning in the complex
relations. We can hypothesize therefore, that they benefit from
their performances in simple situations in order to transpose them to

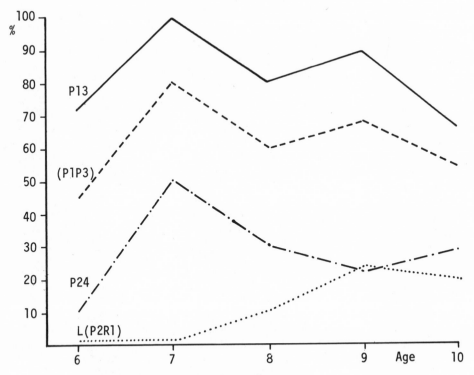

Fig 2.   Comparison: learning and stages.
         ———— At stage 3 for P1 and P3
         –·–·– At stage 3 for P2 and P4
         – – – Generalized learning or no learning needed for
               P1 and P3
         ····· Generalized learning or no learning needed for
               P2 and P4

complex situations.   What we observe later, is a decrease of the
results of level 3, as much for P1, P3 and P2, P4.   Perhaps this is
because the 8-year-old children become more aware of the difficulties
of the situation and yet is still unable to solve it given the fact
that he is not at the formal level of thinking.   In short, this
experiment constitutes a study in itself, since we are clearly able
to distinguish two levels of difficulty – a level concerning simple
perspectives, dealing with simple transformations whose mastery is
characteristic of the concrete operational level of thinking, and a
level of complex transformations whose mastery requires functioning
at a formal level of thinking.   When we ask ourselves what is required in order to make an adequate distinction for all positions,
then we observe that this "trivial" change of the cardboard reference
level was essential.   Furthermore, if we find such a high correlation

between modality of learning, a level of cognitive thinking, and spatial relations, we can clearly say, that spatial relationships are not perceptual which becomes an important argument in regard to cognitive development.

CONCLUSION

Concerning spatial relationships, geometrical drawings and perspectives, it should be noted again that what we have found leads clearly to the hypothesis of generality of cognitive development. Geometrical drawings develop with the same type of evolutions as were observed in Geneva. Furthermore, our Guttmann analysis was able to provide us with a clear indication that topological relationships are as difficult for Geneva children as they are for Oglala children. Euclidean relations begin to appear around five, and the integration of topological and Euclidean relations are only mastered between 5 and 6. Perspectives confirm this similarity of development. Our research which integrated new elements as compared with the Geneva version presented an interesting development and allowed us to retrace not only a similar development between Geneva and Oglala children but also to distinguish between two distinct levels of difficulty: a concrete and a formal one. These two levels are clearly related to the pathway from a complete operational level of thinking, to a formal operational level. Furthermore, our learning modalities are clearly related to the level of operativity which means that even if you do provide the correct solution to the child, he will only make use of it if his cognitive development has achieved a level where he can effectively make use of it. In other words, we have here again a very good example of the strength of operations. In short, our experiment dealing with spatial development, allow us to confirm Piaget's point of view concerning the development of space. As he notes [38] (p.447), "The ordinarily accepted view tends to treat geometrical intuition primarily at a reading or direct perceptual apprehension of the external world, supplemented by images recalling past or anticipating future perceptions." In other words, the usual way to look at the development of space is to look at it as if space would be an intuition. What we have been able to show is that space is an "intuition" neither for Geneva nor for Oglala children. Also, when Piaget notes that [38] (p.484), "An operational system derives its content from a series of abstractions of the subjects action, and not from particular features or properties of the object," that is exactly what we have found here. If simple transformations are succeeded earlier than transformations dealing with complex relationships, then we can say, that as soon as an operational system is complete previously acquired notions begin to crystallize. This is characteristic of the 7-year-old child. As soon as this completion makes possible the mastery of some basic operational properties then new concepts can be integrated. This is not simply the fact of simple addition but leads to a new and complete mental reorganization. If space would be an intuition, then we should find that this intuition is very early acquired, and also that the situation should not be differentiated in terms of the operations involved but only in terms of their perceptual features.

We were able to point out that the situation relative to spatial relationships also implies a relation between a concrete level of thinking, and a certain achievement for simple transformations; for as long as the child does not achieve a formal level of thinking he will not master complex spatial relationships. In other words, the change of reference level and the fact that we introduced learning in our experiment meant nothing as long as it was not embodied in operatory functioning. Clearly the development of space is not space perception but space representation.

DEVELOPMENT OF ELEMENTARY LOGIC

Inclusion of Class

These experiments are described in the book of J. Piaget and B. Inhelder "The Early Growth of Logic in the Child."[27] In our case instead of flowers, we used horses and lions so that the technique is the following.

Material. 12 horses, 2 lions.

Presentation. Ask child to name the animals. One must first be assured that the child has some notion of the class "animals." Ask him to name some animals.

Experiment. (1) Ask child: "How many horses are there?" "How many lions are there?" (As above, it is not necessary that he give the correct number, merely that he recognize that there are more horses than lions.) "Are the horses animals?" Are the lions animals?"

(2) "On this table, do we have more horses or animals - Why?"

(3) "There are 2 children who would like to put together animals. One would like to put together all the horses, the other would like to put together all the lions. Which bunch will be greater?"

(4) "If I give you the horses, what remains in my bunch?" "If I give you the animals, what remains in my bunch?"

(5) "On this table, do we have more animals or horses?" "In the world, do we have more animals or horses?"

In regard to this experiment 4 problems were found:

Question 1: concerns the inclusion itself: "If on the table we see 12 horses and 2 cats, do we have more horses or more animals?"

Question 2: consists in a comparison of subjects: "On this table do we have more horses or more lions?"

Question 3: deals with the subtraction of class: "If the horses were away, what would remain?"

Question 4: quantification of the extension: "In the world do we have more animals, or more horses?" We can schematize the questions in the following manner.

Three stages have been described in the acquisition of the inclusion of class. Stage 1 is called the stage of figural collections. The child cannot differentiate and hence cannot coordinate class comprehension (the sum of the qualities which define membership in a logical class), and extension (the sum of the total objects which possess the given qualities). The child has an ability to form groupings based on the similarities of attributes, which remain dominated by the perceptual configuration. In other words, the child does not master the understanding of "some" and "all" regardless of the context. The quantification of the extension is therefore failed. The quantification of the extension indicates that the child is asked if in the world there are more animals than some specific species in front of his eyes. The subtraction of class is failed as well as the inclusion itself.

At stage 2, we observe difficulties with the comprehension and the extension of class the child tends to unite objects on a similarity of attribute bases alone. He does not maintain a constant, the comprehension of the class and therefore present difficulties in its understanding. Usually one of the three questions is succeeded. In most cases we observe that the child does not have any problems with the subtraction of classes, characteristic of these children is their inability to grasp and keep in mind the inclusion relation and to recognize that the sub-class A is an individual in class B, but does not exhaust it $(A = B - C)$.

On stage 3, we observe logical classification which consists of an operatory coordination between the comprehension and the extension of class. At this point all questions are succeeded.

It is interesting to note the regular progression of stages. At 4, 100% of the subjects are at level 1. None of them achieve either level 2 or 3. One year later, at 5, we still observe a good number of children at level 1 (42%), approximately one-third at level 2, and

another third at level 3. At 6 years, we observe that a majority of
children are at level 2 (62%). This situation remains at 7 years,
where we find 60% at level 2. At 8 years, we have 66% at level 2,
but at 8, none of the children are at level 1, and this remains true
for the rest of our subjects. Between 8 and 9 years, we observe a
clear jump: at 8 years only 30% achieve level 3, whereas at 9 years
90% of the subjects, that is, an overwhelming majority, achieve it.
This situation remains for the 10-year-olds, where we find a majority
(64%) who manifest a level 3. In short, these results indicate that
a regular sequential evolution is followed, despite the highly verbal
nature of the task.

Let us examine the results in terms of stages and by ages.

Table 22. Class Inclusion

Age/Stage	1	2	3
4	100	0	0
5	42	29	29
6	13	62	25
7	10	60	30
8	0	66	34
9	0	10	90
10	0	36	64

Stage 1 Figural collections.
Stage 2 Difficulty with the comprehension and
         the extension of class.
Stage 3 Logical classification.

When we compare these results with Geneva, we observe the following:

Table 23. Inclusion of Classes
(% of success)

Σ = 61	4-5		6		7		8		9	
	O	G	O	G	O	G	O	G	O	G
Inclusion	15	16	38	26	40	46	43	63	82	73
Subtraction	57	43	87	73	80	80	82	83	100	96
Quantification	43	20	63	30	60	53	82	66	100	80

O = Oglala   G = Geneva

We would like to insist, again, that these comparisons are only suggestive. However, it is interesting to note that for question 1, the question of inclusion of class, our 61 subjects performed in the following way: at 4 to 5, when the age groups are organized in the same manner as in Geneva, we find that only 15% of the subjects succeed within the Oglala and 16% within the Geneva group. This comparability of scores remains until age 8, where we find 43% of Oglala succeeding the inclusion as compared with 63% of the Geneva children. At age 9, we find respectively 82% and 73%. For question 3, the subtraction of classes, we observe that we can compare Oglala and Geneva achievement. Between 4 and 5, respectively 57% and 43% succeed the subtraction of class, while at 6, 87% of the Oglala, and 73% of the Geneva correctly answer the question. Subtraction of class, therefore, appears to be much easier than the quantification of the extension, since it is essentially acquired at 6. Thus, we find a jump at the same age for both samples. These results hold for the rest of the children. The question of the quantification of the extension (IV) seems to be succeeded earlier by the Oglala children, in the sense that at each age we observe Oglala children to succeed more often than Geneva children. For example, comparing Oglala with Geneva, we have 57% vs 43% at age 4-5; 63% vs 30% at age 6; 60% vs 53% at 7; 82% vs 66% at 8; and 100% vs 80% at 9. The type of material that we have used seems to have produced some acceleration of the concept of the quantification of the extension, in the sense that even at 6, 63% of the subjects do succeed. Let us note that logical classification is not only one particular operation, but many, namely, inclusion, subtraction, and quantification. When we put the results of all questions together, we obtain the following results.

Table 24.   Inclusion of Classes.
Comparison: Geneva-Oglala

Σ = 61	4-5		6		7		8		9	
	O	G	O	G	O	G	O	G	O	G
Complete success	15	10	25	23	40	43	44	60	71	73
Failure	85	90	75	77	60	57	56	40	29	27

O = Oglala   G = Geneva

Here we observe that the line of success and failure follows the same type of pattern in Geneva and among Oglala children. Between 4-5, 15% of the Oglala and 10% of the Geneva children manifest complete success; at 6 the comparison is 25% vs 23%; at 7, 40% vs 43%;

at 8, 44% vs 60%; and 9, it is 71% vs 73%. We can clearly say that the way logical classification develops follows the same line regardless of the language. It is important to note that some of the Oglala children do not come from an English speaking background. Our findings seem to indicate that logical classification is an operational concept, rather than a linguistic one. We will return to this point later.

There is another aspect of this experiment that we would like to emphasize, namely, the type of material. The material used, which is near the activity of the child has not favored the mastery of logical classification itself. Again, since we have been focusing basic operations and development rather than particular behaviors of development, we have been able to demonstrate that there exists clear similarities between the development of children in Geneva and Oglala. Let us, however, take some examples to further illustrate our point.

> For example, child 407/7, is clearly at stage 1. Here is a conversation that we had with him: "Is horse an animal?" ("Yes") "A cat?" ("No") "What is a cat?" ("I don't know.") "Tell me an animal." (!I cannot know, I can't know anything.") "Tell me an animal you know." ("You can be first.") "Horse." ("Yes") "cat." ("Yes.") "On this table how many lions?" ("Two.") "Horses?" ("Three.") This number is not right. "Are more animals or horses on the table?" ("More horses.") "But, on the table, more lions or more animals?" ("More lions.") This child is clearly on a stage of figural connection where she is unable to make any logical differentiations.

> On another hand, subject 609/29, is clearly at level 2. First of all, she is able to count all the horses. "How many horses?" ("Twelve.") "How many dogs?" ("Two.") "Are horses animals?" ("Yes.") "Are dogs animals?" ("Yes.") "On this table do we have more animals or more horses?" ("More horses.") "How do you know?" ("There are twelve of them.") On the question concerning the quantification of the extension, if asked if in the world there are more horses or more animals she tells us, ("More animals.") "How did you know?" ("I see them.") "On this table do we have more horses or more animals?" ("More horses.") Clearly, in this case the inclusion of class is not succeeded, but this child does not have any problem in solving the subtraction of class. For example, when she is asked, "If I take away all the cats, the horses are going to remain, if I take away all the horses then two dogs are going to remain and if I take away all the animals, then nothing is going to remain." Clearly this child possesses the subtraction of class.

Child 707/37, is at stage 3 for the inclusion of class.
"On this table do we have more horses or more animals?"
("More animals.") "How do you know?" ("They are all
animals.") "In the world do we have more horses or more
animals?" ("More animals.") Furthermore, this child completely succeeds the subtraction of class; moreover,
demonstrates no difficulty with either the quantification
of the extension or the comprehension of the class itself.

The same is true for subject 801/41. "On this table, do we
have more horses or more animals?" ("More animals.") "How
do you know?" ("They have some at ocean and some at zoo.")
"But on the table?" ("More animals.") "In the world, do we
have more horses or more animals?" ("More animals.") "How
do you know?" ("Because there's a lot of them at the
ocean.")

These examples, which are typical of verbal behavior of the
Oglala sample, clearly show that logical classification follows the
same patterns as those observed in Geneva.

Seriation

This experiment has been discussed in the book of Jean Piaget
and Barbel Inhelder, "The Early Growth of Logic in the Child." [27]
Let us describe the technique.

Material. 10 sticks, graduated in 0.5cm steps, from about 10-15cm in
length; 1 intermediary stick, 1 screen.

Presentation. The experimenter gives the sticks to the child and
says: (1) "Make a nice little staircase - place these sticks one
after another from the biggest to the smallest." He notes the way
the child chooses each stick and the order in which it is chosen.
Then he asks, "How did you choose the sticks, what did you do?" (2)
He asks where the intermediate stick must go. (3) The investigator
raises the screen so that child cannot see sticks as they are laid
down, and asks him again to build a staircase or steps. (4) A
counter-suggestion can be used at any point.

We would like to state that our experiment consists of a modification of the technique usually presented, in the sense that we have
used it as a learning experiment to determine the potentiality of the
child. However, in extracting our results we have always dealt with
the spontaneous answers of the children.

Three stages have been described for the acquisition of
seriation. Stage 1, is characterized by a failure in seriation. At
stage 1a, we observe no spontaneous attempts or organize the sticks.

In 1b, we observe that the child does not provide a complete
seriation but constructs small juxtaposed series without a whole
order. In these series we can recognize some couples where the first
element is smaller than the second and sometimes groups of three
sticks correctly seriated, without coordination among the groups.
The child is also able to spontaneously find the smallest stick of
the whole series, and sometimes the longest one. The intermediary
elements are then placed without order and in relation to the ex-
tremes. Sometimes one can also find that the child seriates the
elements according to the top line without taking the bottom line
into account. The child, further, can make no use of the reference
stick, i.e., the intermediary stick, to order them; or he can only do
it partially but is never capable of building the complete seriation.
If the child neglects the bottom part of the sticks, his scale will
be regular only from the point of view of the whole figure constituted by the top line and the sticks will not succeed themselves in
any seriated order. In short, this behavior 1b, is called behavior
dealing with small series, two by two, or three by three. Essentially, the child is not able to build a seriation.

At stage 2, we observe success by groping. For example, the
child begins with small uncoordinated series. At this stage the
child succeeds in building the correct seriation by groping, but he
is unable to make use of a system of relations which enables him to
dominate trial and error, and master the multiple comparisons between
two or three elements. Usually children of this stage fail to place
correctly the intermediary stick or may succeed with groping. In
short, the child of this stage may succeed, but through the use of
groping rather than with an operatory method.

Stage 3, is characterized by an operatory success. At this
stage the child uses a systematic method consisting first of looking
for the smallest or longest element, then the next one and so on.
Only this method is operatory since it shows that a given element B
is simultaneously bigger than the previous one (A –B) and smaller
than the following one (B C). We also observe a spontaneous capacity
to correctly place the intermediary stick without groping.

The point in seriation is not the fact of success or failure,
but the method by which the child achieves it. For instance, it is a
well-known fact that the use of cuisenaire rods has shown this, that
given perceptually large differences between the sticks, the child is
going to succeed. However, the point of our material is to have used
differences which are small enough to force the child to use direct
comparison in order to build his seriation. He cannot do it perceptually; he must deal with the sticks in an operatory way. In this
sense the method used by the child is highly informative in understanding which type of operational stage he is at. Let us observe
first the results obtained by Oglala children.

Table 25.   Elementary Logic.   Experiment: Seriation
A.   By Separate Ages and Stages

71		4	5	6	7	8	9	10
Stage 1	1a	50	0	0	0	0	0	0
	1b	50	70	10	10	0	0	0
Stage 2		0	30	60	30	0	20	9
Stage 3		0	0	30	60	100	80	91

These results are very interesting. For stage 1, we observe
that at age 4, 50% of the subjects are at stage 1a, and 50% at stage
1b. This means that all the 4-year-old children are at stage 1. At
5 years, we observe that even if 70% of the children are still at
stage 1b, 30% are already in stage 2. However, it is interesting to
note that none of the 5-year-old children are at stage 1a. At 6
years the situation is the following: we observe that only 10% of
the children are at stage 1b, 60% are transitional, i.e., have success
through groping, (stage 2) and 30% succeed by an operatory method
(stage 3). Between 6 and 7, we observe a jump. Since at 7 years, if
30% of the subjects are at stage 2, 60% are at stage 3. This situation is maintained for the remaining ages where we find 100% of the
children at stage 3; at 8 years, 80% at 9; and 91% at 10. In short,
we observe that there is a transition of stages through ages. At 4
and 5 all the children are at stage 1, at 6 the majority are transitional, and at 7 the majority succeed through an operatory method.

When we compare out results with those of Geneva, in using the
same categories namely, operatory success, success by groping, small
series, and failure. We observe again there exists a close coordination between both achievements in both populations.

Table 26a.   C. Comparison with Geneva

	4		5		6		7		8-10	
	0	G	0	G	0	G	0	G	0	G
Operatory success	0	0	0	9	30	34	60	63	91	95
Success by groping	0	0	30	12	60	25	30	15	9	5
Small series (2:2)	50	47	70	61	10	34	10	22	0	0
Failure	50	53	0	18	0	7	0	0	0	0

Table 26b. With Intermediate Sticks

| | 4 | | 5 | | 6 | | 7 | | 8-10 | |
	O	G	O	G	O	G	O	G	O	G
Operatory success	0	0	10	9	30	28	70	63	98	95
Partial success	20	20	50	32	70	54	30	37	2	5
Trial	20	20	30	16	0	12	0	0	0	0
No trial	60	60	10	43	0	6	0	0	0	0

At 4, 50% of the children have a behavior of small series, and 50% fail among the Oglalas whereas in Geneva we find 47% and 53% respectively of small series and failure behavior. At 5, we see that the majority of the children in both populations are doing small series: 70% of the children among the Oglala, and 61% among the Geneva children. At 6, we observe that success by groping is charac-teristic of 60% of the Oglala children, as compared with 25% of the Geneva sample. At 6, the percent of children who demonstrate oper-atory success is almost identical for Oglala and Geneva children: 30% and 34% respectively. At 7, we observe the same jump for both popu-lations: 60% of the children of the Oglala manifest an operatory success as compared with 63% of the Geneva children. Between 8 and 10, 91% of the Oglala children are operatory as compared with 95% in Geneva. Moreover, none of the children in either population display complete failure or small series behavior. In short, we see that these results parallel what we have already observed: strong simi-larities in patterns of development between the Oglala and Geneva samples.

The results in terms of the child's behavior with the intermedi-ary stick are also informative. No trial at placing the reference stick is characteristic of 60% of both populations at age 4. At 5, 50% of the Oglala children and 32% of the Geneva children achieve partial success; 30% and 16% respectively make a trial of placing the intermediary stick, and 10% and 43% still manifest no attempt to place the stick. At 6, we observe that the majority of the children in Geneva and Oglala display partial success in placing the inter-mediary stick: 70% vs 54% respectively, whereas at 7, 8, 9, and 10, the majority of the children demonstrate operatory success in cor-rectly placing the intermediary stick. This behavior of finding the correct position for the intermediary stick is important because it enables us to better understand the method by which the child suc-ceeds. Moreover, it helps us in understanding if the child is really operatory. For example, once the seriation is completed, let us assume by groping, then the child usually continues to display the same type of method in order to find the correct place for the intermediary stick. Some children completely destroy their series in order to put the intermediary stick in the correct place. However, when a child is operatory, he has no difficulty in directly discovering the correct place for the intermediary stick.

In the experiment on seriation we have considered the types of learning displayed, and we have distinguished the same type of modalities as have been described in the section of spatial relationships, as the examination of Table 27 reveals.

Table 27. B. Learning

	4	5	6	7	8	9	10
N	70	10	0	0	0	0	0
L	30	70	40	20	0	0	0
M	0	20	30	20	0	20	10
NL	0	0	30	60	100	20	100

N = No learning.
L = Local learning (2:2;2:3).
M = More than 2:2; or 2:3 generalized learning.
NL = Needs no learning.

We differentiated between no learning, (N) a local learning; (L) (the child is able to integrate small and big, or small medium and big and so on, that is, two by two and two by three), the display of more than two by two or a generalized learning; (M) finally he may not need any learning at all (NL). Interestingly, we find almost a superimposition of the modality of learning and their operatory stage. That is, the child is unable to learn more than what his operatory level allows him to do. For example, at 4, we observe that 100% of the children are at stage 1, with 70% at stage 1b; among them, 70% manifest no learning and (N). 30% display a type of local learning (L), but none of them go further. Most of the children who are able to demonstrate local learning are not able to enhance their performance in the direction of a higher level of operativity. In other words, even if one can provide the child with information that he can use, within a given context, such as seriation, he is not going to surpass his performance; rather one must wait for his operatory structure to develop to see incidence of other modalities of learning. For the 6-year-old children, 40% display local learning, whereas, 60% of them either need no learning or display generalized learning to complete the task. In particular, those children who manifest an operatory method in the construction of the seriation do not need any learning, whereas those who succeed by groping demonstrate either a local learning (L), or generalized learning (M). At 8, we observe that there are no children for whom learning is necessary to successfully complete the seriation; this is also characteristic of the majority of 9 and 10 year olds. In short, our learning experiment was not a real learning procedure although it strongly illustrates the analogy between the ability to integrate information and an operatory level of thinking. This is precisely what we found in space.

CONCLUSION

The importance of elementary logic has been recognized by psychology for a long time. The majority of studies dealing with elementary logic have been well reviewed by Vinacke [39]. Nevertheless, until Piaget had published his book, comparatively little had been done relative to the study of the origin or classificatory behavior in children. Such research as that provided by Hazlitt [40], or Annett [41], were limited to an empirical determination of the extent to which children are able to classify at different ages. However, the experiments of Piaget seek to penetrate more deeply into the psychological mechanisms underlying the development of classificatory and ordering behavior in a large number of situations. In other words, this type of experiment deals with an explanation of classificatory behaviors rather than with simply a description of children's behavior. That was one of our concerns in choosing elementary logic. Piaget and Inhelder were particularly concerned with establishing the precise relation between the classifications of children and the kinds of interferences they make on the basis of these classifications. Inclusion of class and seriation are complimentary in many ways. Whereas the inclusion of class if highly verbal, seriation seems largely perceptual. We observe however, that both seriation and the inclusion are achieved at approximately the same age; the implication is that there is a relationship between the mastery of both tasks.

VI

Appraisal of Results

One of the problems which arises from our research is the concept of continuity and discontinuity of cognitive development. Piaget makes clear that we observe a functional continuity and a structural discontinuity in cognitive development by functional continuity we mean for example, that one can find in sensorimotor intelligence, the practical equivalence of classes and of relations which later are going to be constructed on an abstract level.

But from the point of view of this structure, that is to say the efficiency of the system the fact remains that between sensorimotor coordination and abstract conceptual coordination fundamental differences arise which deal with the nature of intellectual growth.

The problem of equilibrium is relevant here. As we have insisted earlier, there are two important properties of thinking which have to be distinguished: states and transformations. In doing this, however, we must elucidate two main questions. First is the question of the factors which drive the intellectual ability in general to operatory structures; this is essentially a problem of equilibrium. Second is the problem of the factors which connect operatory structures to one another; this is a problem of transformation, or better, of the relations of the structures.

To determine the conditions of the genesis of cognitive development is to know essentially how whole operations arrive at an equilibrated state, and more precisely to know the laws of this particular equilibrium.

On the level of the simple perception of the practical or sensorimotor intelligence, and of the pre-operational period of thinking thought does not reach a permanent equilibrium; this is because reasoning does not constitute a real structure. In other words, reasoning modifies itself, periodically changes its structure and is partially or totally affected by the experience. The contradictions between the anticipations and the obtained result create the need to transform the original belief. For this reason we observe successive phases of equilibrium and disequilibrium, which are the main characteristics of the first stages of cognitive development.

Having been able to demonstrate the succession of stages it is now time to understand what we mean by functional continuity and a structural discontinuity. Usually the concrete operational period of thinking begins to appear around the age 6-7, and is achieved around 8-9. That is, around 8-9 the child arrives at a state of equilibrium. If we consider the results obtained for Oglala children, we observe the following:

Table 28

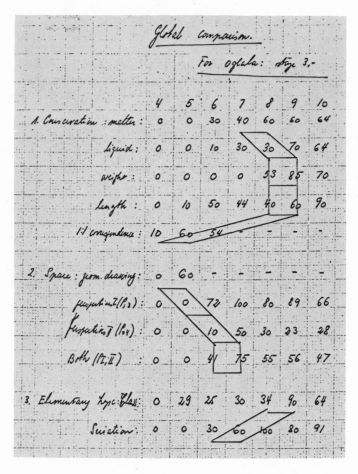

What we see here are the characteristics of stage 3 functioning, the stage of operational thinking for Oglala children. Concerning conservation of matter, we observe that the jump from a minority of children demonstrating operative reasoning to a majority of children demonstrating operative functioning, is situated between 7 and 8. At seven there are 40% of the children who think in operational terms with a majority of them functioning pre-operationally, while at eight the majority (60%) think in operative terms. For conservation of liquid we observe that the jump comes between 8 and 9. At 8, 30% of the children are at level 3, at 9, 70%. For weight and length also we observe that the jump is between 8 and 9, weight 53% vs. 45% and length 40% vs. 60%. The one-to-one correspondence is achieved much earlier. It is usually mastered between 4 and 5 and is achieved around 6. The interesting point here is that three jumps occur between 8 and 9, the age which corresponds to the consolidation of operative thinking. Matter seems to proceed the acquisition of liquid, length, and weight.

In space the picture is the following. For geometrical drawings we observe a leap between 4 and 5 as is seen in the development of the one-to-one correspondence. None of the children are at stage 3 at 4, while 60% of the children are at level 3 at age 5. For perspectives if we distinguish between concrete transformations and complex ones we observe that the former are achieved at 6, where already 70% of the children are at level 3, whereas the latter are not even achieved at 9 (28%) with a 50% at 7.

In elementary logic we observe that the main jump is between 8 and 9, where we have 34% of the children at 8 and 90% at 9 who are at stage 3. Seriation is achieved between 6 and 7, from 30% at 6 to 60% at 7, who are at level 3. In short, it is between 6, 7 and 8 that all the main leaps are observed. Briefly, in our nine experiments, four (almost a majority) demonstrate a clear jump between 8 and 9 from a level where the child doubts his conservation to a level where he is completely operational. This concerns three experiments dealing with logical invariances: length, weight, and liquid, and one experiment dealing with elementary logic: inclusion of class. One conservation is achieved between 4 and 5, the one-to-one correspondence and the geometrical drawings; one experiment between 5 and 6, simple perspective; seriation is mastered between 6 and 7, whereas complex transformations are not completely achieved even at 10.

These results clearly demonstrate that there is a regular succession of stages, and leads us to the problem of the discontinuity of structures which is the second aspect of the problem of the transformations which we have introduced earlier. These transformations assure the pathway from an equilibrated form of organization to another one. This last refers mainly to the problem of the time delay.

We can distinguish between two types of time delay. The first one concerns vertical time delays, or in logical terms, time delays in comprehension where we have the same system of concepts which drive to two successive organizations or distinct levels of psychological activity. For instance, at the sensorimotor level the child realizes the constitution of a practical space, and later the constitution of a representative space. The second one concerns horizontal time delays or time delays in extension which occur when the same concept must be enlarged to include many contents as is the case, for instance, in conservation. Various forms of conservation (matter, weight, etc.) are achieved at different times by the same child.

During the pre-operational level we see that there are two types of transformations which we observed in our results. The first consists in the acquisition of what we will call basic spatial features. In particular, if the child acquires between 4 and 5 both Euclidean and topological relations as it is the case in the geometrical drawings, then it is clear that he begins to understand transformational features of space. This process begins by an initial discrimination of topological relations, later of Euclidean relations and finally of their integration. In other words, here we observe a reconstruction dealing with the use and constitution of the abstraction of geometrical relations. This construction completed, the child can begin to work on such problems as representative space which leads to the further construction of simple perspectives. The essence of a rational spatial coordination is then to be sought in the logic of relations, that is, in the fundamental group of operations which assure the reciprocity of individual perspectives and the relativity of the fact of experience. It is evident and our results support it, that it is the logic of relations which makes the child gradually come to understand (between 7 and 10 years) that the left and the right are not absolutes, that his own left corresponds to the right of an individual opposite him, and that an object between two others is at the same time at the left of the first and at the right of the third. It is thus the logic of relations which permits the formation of the idea of a conceptual space, by a coordination of the different possible perspectives which allows the imposition of this construction upon practical space whose relationships are always limited to one's own perspective. Furthermore, if we take into account our results in seriation where we observe that it is between 6 and 7 that the child achieves operatory functioning, and is able to master logical relations, then its impact upon complex perspectives becomes clear, for we have a majority of children who succeed the seriation while only a few can transpose it to complete success in spatial relations dealing with complex transformations. In other words, we see here reasons for the time delay in the reconstruction that we observe is not directly deduced from the child's success in mastering Euclidean and topological relations. Something more has to be added which comes from the logic of relations. In short, we do not see any direct continuity, at least in a structural sense, between the mastery of geometrical drawings and the mastery of spatial relations.

This leads us to a possible explanation of why we have found that perspectives were so difficult even for 9- and 10-year-old children. The reason does not really differ from that of the conditions of equilibrium because the same notion can give many successive constructions. The reason is that pre-operational thinking is not sufficient to provide a stable equilibrium.

In regard to the second type of time delay we have found that children achieve the conservation of matter before they achieve the conservation of weight and liquid. The main pathway for matter is between 7 and 8, for liquid and weight between 8 and 9. But what does this implication represent on a psychological level? This is the main problem, and again the logical problems of the successive coordinations drives us to an important psychological question, dealing with the mechanism of equilibrium. The equilibrium of actions and operations can be characterized by three distinct qualities. First, the dimension of its field, second, its flexibility, and third, its stability.

The first point refers to the field of activity within which the equilibrium is possible. We observe that during development the "surface" of this field grows with every new step in development. To say it simply, the spatial temporal trajectory between the subject and the object grows in complexity at every change of level.

For the second point, if the field of the equilibrium extends itself gradually to arrive finally at the point of including all possible activities, flexibility grows in correlation. For instance, a child who possesses only the one-to-one correspondence will have a flexibility of thinking which will be more restricted than that he will have after he masters all logical invariances dealing with conservation and elementary logic.

Finally, at the same time that the equilibrium becomes more flexible it acquires a greater stability. For instance, with the acquisitional sensorimotor intelligence this stability is already increased since objects can be found again; with pre-operational thought there is yet another increase in stability because they begin to be able to be anticipated. But it is only with operatory intelligence that this stability is really assured since empirical reversibility (the active possibility of return) is replaced by a true and constant reversibility (the abstract understanding of it).

The fact that we observe that Oglala children achieve operational thinking between 8 and 9, as is reported in Geneva, is an important feature. In order to understand further the similarities of the sequence of stages let us now deal with a global comparison for all experiments between Oglala and Geneva children.

Table 29. Global Comparison: Pre-Operating Level (stage 1) for all Experiments compared with Geneva

	4		5		6		7		8		9		10	
	O	G	O	G	O	G	O	G	O	G	O	G	O	G
1 Conservation: matter	100	–	83	84	40	68	50	64	10	24	24	12	–	–
liquid	100	–	100	15	40	40	40	4	10	2	–	–	–	–
weight	–	–	–	–	–	–	–	–	31	40	15	16	10	16
length	94	92	94	92	50	96	55	80	60	32	20	4	–	–
1:1 correspondence	90	92	40	50	46	25	–	–	–	–	–	–	–	–
2 Space: geom. drawings	50	–	0	–	–	–	–	–	–	–	–	–	–	–
perspectives	–	–	–	–	–	–	81	100	63	87	68	74	63	57
3 Elementary Logic: class	85	90	85	90	75	77	60	57	56	40	29	27	–	–
seriation (a) small series	50	47	70	61	10	34	10	22	0	0	–	–	–	–
(b) failure	50	53	0	18	0	7	0	0	0	0	–	–	–	–

O = Oglala children
G = Geneva children

– Not available

These results are interesting in the sense that they indicate a repartition of level 1, at the same ages for both samples in almost all experiments. We observe that the majority of the children are at level 1, at 5 years for matter (83% for Oglala children and 84% in Geneva), and for length (94% for Oglalas and 92% in Geneva). We observe a decrease in the frequency of level 1 from 4 until 7, for both samples. For example, in length, if 94% of the Oglalas and 92% of the Geneva children are at level 1, at 5 years, only 20% and 4% respectively are still at this level at 9. This corresponds to an increase of level 2 and later of level 3.

For the one-to-one correspondence both samples have a majority at level 1 at 4 (90% and 92% respectively). For geometrical drawings, again, even if there are no comparisons available with Geneva in terms of stages, we observe that the majority of the children are at level 1. For simple perspectives we observe a decrease of level 1, from age 7 to 10. If among Oglala and Geneva children at 7, we find 81% and 100% respectively functioning at level 1, a year later, we find 63% of the Pine Ridge children and 87% of the Geneva children still at level 1; at 9 years, 68% and 74% respectively followed by 63% and 67% respectively at 10. Clearly the behavior of both samples is similar in its tendencies.

For elementary logic, in class inclusion we observe that still at 7-8; 60% and 57% of the children are clearly at level 1, manifesting difficulties in differentiating between the comprehension and the extension of the class. Again, we observe a decrease of level 1, from 4 to 8. If 85% of the Oglala and 90% of the Geneva children are at level 1 at 4, at 9 it is characteristic of only a minority in each sample (29% and 27% respectively).

Seriation is interesting when we compare the differences between small series and failure. Failure is the characteristic of the majority of 4-year-old children (54% of the Oglala and 53% of Geneva) but success in small series is characteristic of the majority of 5-year-old children (70% of Oglala children and 61% for Geneva).

In short, the repartition of the pre-operational level of stage 1, demonstrates a similarity of patterns of behavior between Oglala and Geneva children. In the nine experiments, we observed that the 4- and 5-year-old children are all pre-operational. The 6-year-old children are characterized in both samples by a marked decrease of level 1, and an increase in the incidence of level 2 and 3 and so on.

We are now going to compare the operatory level 3, for all our experiments in Geneva.

We observe as noted earlier in the analysis of Table 28, that in all experiments the two samples are almost equivalent. In conservation of matter it is at 8 years that 60% of Oglala children and 72%

Table 30. Global Comparison: Operatory Level (3) for all Experiments Compared with Geneva

	4		5		6		7		8		9		10	
	O	G	O	G	O	G	O	G	O	G	O	G	O	G
1 Conservation: matter	0	0	0	16	30	16	40	32	60	72	62	84	-	-
liquid	0	0	0	4	10	18	30	74	55	87	-	-	-	-
weight	0	0	0	0	0	0	0	0	53	52	85	72	70	76
length	0	0	6	8	50	4	45	20	40	68	80	96	-	-
1:1 correspondence	10	8	60	50	54	75								
2 Space: geom. drawing	0	-	60	-	0	0	19	0	37	13	32	26	37	43
perspectives	0	0	0	0	0									
3 Elementary Logic: class	15	10	15	10	25	23	40	43	44	60	71	73	-	-
seriation	0	0	0	9	30	34	60	63	91	95	-	-	-	-

of Geneva children achieve it. For liquid, 74% of the Geneva children achieve it at 7, and 55% of the Oglala at 8. For weight, we have at 8, 53% of Oglala children and 53% for Geneva. For length, the 8-year-old Geneva children show 68% as compared with 80% of the Oglala children at 9. For the one-to-one correspondence both samples again intersect at the same age (5), (50% vs. 60%). For perspectives, again both samples intersect at 10, with 37% for Oglala and 43% for Geneva children. For the inclusion of class we observe that if 60% of the Geneva children achieve it at 8, 71% of the Oglala children achieve it at 9. For seriation both samples achieve it at 7, 60% and 63% respectively.

For five of nine experiments we have a clear superimposition of the age and the operatory level.

These are the main results. Their appraisal leads us to a clear understanding of the similarity of the succession of stages for both samples.

VII

Pedagogical Implications

Again and again our results have revealed a deep relationship between operatory development and certain modalities of learning. This deep relationship between the way in which a child integrates information and the stage of his operational development are more and more recognized as important for education. And yet there remains controversy around the possibility of teaching certain fundamental operations.

Most of the results in learning experiments have shown most clearly that logic as such cannot be taught. Most of the results agree with the following: if a child is purely pre-operational, that is, if his belief changes according to transformations; if he is convinced that the quantity of matter changes with changes in the perceptual appearance, there is little probability that he can be made to change his point of view. For instance, Mimi Sinclair, in one of her more recent researches [42], and Barbel Inhelder [42] have been able to show the extreme difficulties involved in providing the child with a change of stages.

Further, most of the results clearly agree with the fact that if a child is already transitional, that is at stage 2, the level at which he manifests vacillation of thinking, it then becomes much easier to introduce and make him aware of other possibilities, including operatory solutions. In other words, the type of learning which works, is a type of learning which pushes rather than a type of learning which changes the point of view of the subject.

Where learning is defined as new knowledge derived from experience with particular events, physical abstraction illustrates learning in its dependence upon generalized knowledge realized by means of

formal abstraction. According to this definition and to the definition of Piaget, the development of general intelligence is not a
process of learning, but a process of equilibration through formal
abstraction. This statement does not deny the biological necessity
of a physical or social environment, but merely specifies the manner
in which general and particular knowledge grow in the person's interaction with the environment. In this case it becomes interesting to
see which type of focus can be given to our results with Oglala
children.

We have insisted in the discussion of the results, that a problem of sequential equilibration is at the heart of the controversies
in learning. What does this mean? The problem of equilibration
dealing with vertical as well as horizontal time delays as those we
observe in conservation, for example, clearly lead to the idea that
cognitive contradictions are important in the development of intelligence. It should be noted that M. Bovet [6], in her experiments
dealing with Algerian children, observed that some children who were
impermeable to cognitive contradictions, remained at the stage of
pseudo-conservation until made aware of the contradiction between
their own point of view and that of reality. Then they became pre-
operational and started to move toward operational functioning.
Thus, one important fact, is permeability to contradiction. This
leads us to particular teaching procedures which can be of value in
the education of the children of our population. Let us first, however, assess some general points.

Many questions have arisen concerning the distinction between a
prospective or functional point of view and a structural or retro-
spective point of view concerning the development of intelligence.
As Piaget stated in one of his newly published books [43] (p.249)

"for sure we observe an evolution of the answers which
seems to provide a structural transformation of thinking
with age, but if one compares as a whole the reaction of
small children to older children, it is not possible to
admit that there is not an evolution" (Author's translation).

It is precisely one of the fundamental aspects of our research
to have shown this basic transformation of thinking as present in
Oglala children as it is in Geneva. However, as we have always been
careful to warn the reader concerning the meaning of the numbers and
percentages quoted, it is important to note that the characteristic
ages one obtains even with a great number of children are only means.
The succession, even if globally realistic, does not exclude the
intersection of individual temporary regressions. This is important
in teaching where we must assess the possibility of functioning continuity in development parallel by structural discontinuity. Furthermore, we have noted earlier the types of time delays which may be

present in the acquisition of a concept, and in our discussion of the results, we have clearly stated which type of time delay we were referring to, vertical or horizontal; but our point is not really to generate generalities about cognitive contradiction, but to capture spirit of the synthesis that Piaget describes. In other words, the type of contradictions to which we are referring are cognitive ones, essentially dealing with the anticipation of the child and his observation of this anticipation.

When we observe that there exists a conflict between the expectation and an unexpected obstacle, we ask ourselves how the child solves this problem. What means are open to the child? This is an important question for pedagogy. Several possibilities are open. In the first place, the child may try to correct his assumption. For example, he may try to take the exceptions into account, to explain them and to fix the meaning of his assumption within the new limits thus set. This is one way, but it means that the child is already aware that a contradiction exists between his anticipation and the obtained results. This does not seem to be the case with children who are purely pre-operational, those who believe that the world changes.

In the second place, the child might try to overcome the obstacle itself by defining clearly its significance. Thus, for instance, faced with a new reality which disconcerts his anticipation, the child may ask several relevant questions concerning the nature of this obstacle, thereby clarifying the significance of the obstacle which lies between his expectation, and the observed results. Already these two methods open many means to establishing a meaningful pedagogy for each child.

In the third place, the child may differentiate his schema, by dividing an original law into two with each thus constituted requiring more or less independent explanations.

There appears to be a more radical solution, that in which the original anticipation is recognized as false, and the mind is directed toward new schemas. This procedure seems to be particularly important when we want to see a child move from a pre-operational level of thinking to a logical one.

But there exists a fifth possibility. When the mind is incapable of discovering new laws with which it might circumvent the obstacle, it may as a last resort, come back upon itself and revise its method. In other words, its activity hitherto directed toward the outside world, may now include in addition, a becoming aware of the method followed, a reflection upon that method, and finally an effort to revise it. Such is the character of cognitive activity, and therefore of the type of teaching which generally should be provided for children: a progressive organization of experience proceeding by way of extension, revision, and differentiation of anticipated schemas, for instance, by simultaneous coordination of facts and methods. In other words, instead of directing learning towards the acquisition of new facts, one should emphasize in any teaching procedure, the method by which the child is able to move toward a solution. Our results indicate that this method has a good probability of success. Learning in this sense is more than a pouring of facts into the mind of the child; it is, a methodological discovery as well as a progressive reorganization through which the child is able to overcome his own pre-operational manner of functioning.

For example, in an attempt to prepare pre-school children for the acquisition of elementary number concepts, Constance Kami [44] makes some important points concerning the concept and the development of certain basic operatory ideas. The main point of Kami, which we would like to make ours, is the following. A basic Piagetian principle is that the concept of number, for example, is achieved as a result of the structuring of the underlying processes and not vice-versa. Therefore, the teaching procedures outlined by Kami [45] and by Piaget himself, carefully avoid the imposition of conservation and include only activities which aim at strengthening the underlying processes. This distinction is important because in strengthening the underlying process, the child will better be able to achieve the one particular concept.

The teaching procedures which we will describe are seen as a vacillation of the transition from sensory-motor intelligence, to operational intelligence. That is to say, they are particularly feasible for this transitional stage called the pre-operational period. At this time the child begins to systematize his physical and social knowledge, to construct logical structures, and to rebuild on a representational level the practical knowledge he has acquired during the sensory-motor period. We are going to outline, according to our results teaching procedures in three important domains. First, logico-mathematical relationships, dealing with classification, seriation, and number, then conservation, and finally spatial and temporal relationships [46].

PRACTICAL RECOMMENDATIONS

In presenting our practical recommendations we are replying mainly upon the point of view of Kami and so we will quote rather extensively her text:

A. Logico-Mathematical Relationships

While each specific object was all important in the teaching of physical knowledge, the particular objects do not matter in the teaching of logico-mathematical relationships. What matters is the relationship among the objects. For example, grouping according to

function is not tied to pencils, items of clothing, or foods. Therefore, a large variety of objects should be available for the child to
group, to order, and to count.

1. Classification

From the first day of school, at clean-up time, the children can
put together things that are the same and separate those that are
different. Games can be developed for them to find identical objects
from an array of grossly different things (e.g. two cups, two
sponges, and three crayons). Sorting games in which the children
find identical objects by touch alone also strengthens awareness of
similarities and differences.

Grouping identical objects is relatively easy, and the children
soon become ready to group together things that are not exactly the
same. Three types of reasons for grouping can be discerned from
Piaget's theory. The first and easiest type is by situational belonging, e.g. the placement of a cake of soap with a washrag, and a man's
shirt with a necktie. Grouping by situational belonging is based on
spatial proximity, which is the child's first principle of unifi-
cation. The second type of grouping is based on what the child does
with the objects, e.g. the placement of a white crayon with a white
pencil, and a cigarette with a white straw. The third type of grouping is by abstraction from the objects themselves, e.g. the placement
of the cigarette with the crayon ("because they are both short"), and
the straw with the pencil ("because they are both long"). Grouping
by color, shape, size, and material are other examples of grouping by
abstraction from the objects.

Kits can be put together containing objects that can be grouped
according to any of the above principles. The objects used should be
those with which the children have already played in school or at
home. It is important to remember in the teaching of classification
that there is no right or wrong grouping, since how the objects are
grouped is determined by the child's wish. In physical knowledge, the
outcome of an action is determined entirely by the object. A metal
ball cannot be flattened no matter how hard the child tries. In
classification, on the other hand, the outcome of the action is
determined by what the child wants. If he wants to group objects by
length, this response is just as correct as grouping them according
to function or color.

2. Seriation

The simplest seriation task involves sizes (e.g. the big, the
bigger, and the biggest glass). A prerequisite for seriation according to size is the ability to make comparisons between two sizes. To
teach this skill, it is necessary to begin with dichotomies of
grossly different sizes of the same object (e.g. big and little

square blocks). Similar tasks can be built into the program to per-
meate the entire day. At first, equipment in all the activity areas
can be provided in only two sizes. In the doll corner, the children
use and arrange big and little pots, plates, spoons, dolls, etc. The
block and truck area has shelves with two sizes of blocks, cars,
trucks, and animal figures. In art, big and little brushes and paper
are used. At juice time, cups and cookies can be of two different
sizes. On the playground, children can take big and little steps,
make long and short shadows, swing on swings of two sizes and
heights, and play with big and little balls and hoops.

Later on in the school year, when two sizes have been mastered,
the environment is enriched so that children can order objects of
three or more sizes. Objects such as nesting cups and blocks are
particularly good for beginning the ordering of many sizes because of
their self-corrective nature.

Comparisons can be taught about other qualities as well, such as
hardness and loudness. These activities also begin with gross differences and insure that the children will be able to act on objects to
compare their salient quality (e.g. learning about "hard" and "soft"
by pressing down on a block and a piece of foam rubber having the
same shape, size, and color). Rhythmics and instruments can be used to
compare different degrees of loudness. Again, it is important that a
large variety of materials and sensorimotor activities be used in
the teaching of the prerequisites for seriation, as the essence of
seriation is a system of relative differences which should not be
tied to a few limited objects.

3. Numbers

The basic number goal in pre-school for the teaching of numbers
is to help the child construct a foundation for a logical system of
numbers based on one-to-one correspondence, so that he will overcome
his tendency to quantify a set of objects by the size of the space
they occupy. The first strategy in helping the child to overcome his
tendency to use space for numerical quantification is the establishment of equivalence by "provoked" one-to-one correspondence. "Provoked correspondence" uses two homogeneous sets which correspond
qualitatively with each other in such a way that there can be only
one element of a set to correspond with an element in the other set
(e.g. a set of houses to correspond with a set of roofs). In using
provoked correspondence, the teacher can ask the child to "find
enough roofs for all the houses" without using words like "the same
number" or "as many as," which the child often cannot understand.
The qualitative correspondence between the house and the roof facili-
tates the child's establishment of one-to-one correspondence.

A second way to help the child overcome his tendency to base
numerical judgment on space is through the teaching of linear ordering. This activity involves two identical sets of heterogeneous

objects (e.g. a toy sock, shoe, dress, hat, etc). Children are asked to make a copy of one of the sets arranged in a line. Interest can be added by having the children put paper clothes on a "clothesline" to look just like the teacher's line, or on a shelf to look just like the teacher's shelf. Linear ordering focuses the child on each object separately and prevents him from basing his judgment on the space occupied.

When children can establish numerical equivalence by one-to-one correspondence, games involving addition and subtraction are played. For example, after the child finds as many cups as saucers, the teacher adds an extra cup and asks him whether there are now enough saucers for all the cups, and what he should do to have enough. The child should be asked to justify his answer by his own manipulation of objects. If he decides that there are more cups than saucers, he will put one cup on (or next to) each saucer, and either take away the extra cup or add an extra saucer.

When a child can firmly establish equivalence, the teacher can change the spatial configuration of the sets and ask the child whether or not there are now enough saucers for all the cups. The next question about conservation is "How do you know?"

B. Conservation

The teaching strategy for children who do not have conservation is the development of "renversabilité" (empirical reversibility). "Renversabilité" is prepared for at the sensorimotor level by the child's arranging sets of object in one configuration (e.g. ten cups in a line), disarranging them (the same cups in a pile), and then re-arranging them back to their original configuration. This practical knowledge can be used and extended in pre-school by having the child begin considering such questions as "This doll wants to have a party. Put all the saucers in a line and then take out enough cups for all the saucers ... Now, the doll wants to wash the cups; so put all the cups in a pile ... Now, the cups are clean. Do you think you can put them back the way they were before? Do you think there will be a cup for each saucer? Let's put the cups back and see." This kind of activity is carried out numerous times using a large variety of different objects. Using dramatic play in number games has been found helpful in creating greater interest and involvement for the children.

A fundamental point to be gleaned from Piaget's theory of number is the importance of the child's own action on objects. It is essential in all the activities described above that the child himself carry out the actions at all times. Games establishing or judging the numerical equivalence of two sets that the teacher arranged do not provide the full educational experience. Again, it is important that numerical equivalence not be tied to a few limited objects.

C. Infra-Logical (spatio-temporal) Relationships

1. Spatial Relationships

Three directions of programming can be discerned from Piaget's writings on spatial concepts. One aspect of development is the child's structuring of space from topological space to geometric space. Another aspect is the development of static space into more dynamic transformations. The third aspect is the reconstruction of sensorimotor space on a representational level.

Traditional topological spatial relationships such as "on", "off", "in", and "out" are taught through a sequence involving (a) motoric coordination with self-to-object relationships (e.g. getting on a block), (b) motoric coordination with object-to-object relationships (e.g. making a doll get on the block), and (c) motoric coordination of body parts in relation to each other (e.g. putting a finger on the nose).

An example of spatial transformation is that involving part-whole relationships. In order to learn part-whole transformations, the children disassemble objects into component parts, and reassemble them to their original form. An example is the cutting of apples into two, three, or four pieces and reassembling the proper pieces into the original apples. The "Fruit Bowl" marketed by Creative Playthings and construction toys such as tinker toys and Creative Snap Blocks are also useful for making three-dimensional part-whole transformations. Puzzles are ready-made materials for two-dimensional transformations, and the cutting up and pasting together of pictures and geometric shapes also teach spatial transformations. The most convincing evidence of the static nature of the four-year-old's space is his inability to reassemble a simple square that he has just cut into three pieces.

The four-year-old's sensorimotor space has developed into geometric space, but on the representational plane he tends to be still at the topological level. When he is asked to find another square (a perceptual task), the four-year-old can easily do this task. However, when he is asked to copy a square (a representational task), he is likely to produce either a circle or a kind of circle having one or two angles.

Two strategies may help the child to structure his representational space more geometrically. One is a variety of mystery-box games using perception by touch alone. When the child cannot see a shape, he is forced to structure his mental image of the shape. The other strategy is a variety of rhythmics activities involving the imitation of the teacher's body movements. When the child has to imitate the extending of one arm forward and the other arm to the side, for example, he has to mentally structure the 90° angle and the parallel of both arms in relation to the floor, thereby strengthening his geometric notions on the representational place. Watching the movements of his body in a wide, full-length mirror has been found helpful to the child who has difficulty in these activities. The structuring of body image, too, results from imitation of body movements. Having the child assemble the pieces of a puzzle is by comparison not an effective way to teach body image.

Linear ordering has already been mentioned in connection with the teaching of numbers. This activity involves representation (i.e. copying) of topological relationships (i.e. the coordination of proximities, or the coordination of the relationship "next to"). While straight copying does not involve any transformation, two variations of linear ordering do. One such variation is ordering in a longer or shorter line than the model. For example, the teacher can put two sheets at both ends of the child's laundry line and ask him to hang up his clothes in exactly the same way as the teacher, even though his line has less empty space. The second variation is inverse order. In this task, the child is asked to begin with the last item of the teacher's line and end up with the first item of the model.

2. Temporal Relationships

It has been stated in the accompanying "framework" paper that it is appropriate to try to structure the four-year-old's time into sequences but not into intervals. Another appropriate goal is the notion of speed at the sensorimotor level.

The school day offers numerous occasions for teaching sequence with the children's own activities. Some sequence involved large intervals, such as the daily schedule of going outside and the having juice, while others involve brief specific activities (e.g. planning together the sequence of clean-up). Rhythmics and large-motor activities are particularly good for games emphasizing temporal sequence, as these enable children to experience sequence in a vivid sensorimotor way (e.g. touching the eyes, the shoulders, and then the feet).

The preceding sequences are arbitrary and therefore devoid of real meaning. Piaget points out that the notion of temporal sequence grows out of casual relationships, and vice versa. Thus, a good way to teach temporal sequence is in combination with the teaching of physical knowledge. For example, the action of dropping a ball precedes its bouncing. The means-end relationship, too, is a meaningful way to teach temporal sequence. For example, the children are asked what they have to do to make a big piece of paper for a big painting when only little pieces are available. Socio-dramatic play is another way of teaching temporal order in a meaningful way. For example, the children have to buy their "groceries" before they start "cooking".

Speed is taught only in the sense of acting either slowly or fast in rhythmics. "Walk across the walking board as fast (or as slowly) as you can" is an example of the level that the children can understand. Pounding on the table faster, faster, and faster is another example, which has implications for the learning of seriation.

The question remains why these techniques are important. Our results among Oglala children show us that the general patterns they follow are the same as are observed in Geneva. For example, the one-to-one correspondence is acquired for both samples much earlier than is classification, seriation, and number. It appears to be the case that the one-to-one correspondence is a prerequisite for the constitution of classification and seriation as much as classification and seriation are prerequisites for the understanding of the concept of number. In short, teaching should lead not exclusively to learning procedures, or the gain of knowledge, but should be oriented primarily to the construction of organizational means in order to achieve an operatory level. Certainly classification and seriation are both recognized as basic, whereas the one-to-one correspondence, the putting of different objects into corresponding relationships has not been emphasized enough in the new teaching approaches. In particular, most of the studies done among disadvantaged populations tend to emphasize biological and psychophysiological features to explain their lack of intellectual development. Of course, biological needs must be fulfilled, but around 4, 5, and 6 the type of basic acquisitions that the child usually achieves through a stimulating environment should be supplied by a meaningful environment at school if the family does not provide it. For example, at the Pine Ridge Reservation, one of the things which should be done to enhance the underlying cognitive development of children, would be to have some types of organizational means to get to children as early as possible. PCC in its new form, could be a very important way to help very young children overcome obstacles and develop their native abilities in achieving correspondences and later classification, seriation, and so on. Certainly it is an important problem to be able to reach those children where the family conditions are insufficient to provide the conditions of good development. In most of the cases, for example, when we speak of pseudo-mental retardation, we are really referring to the child who did not have in the beginning of his life the possibility of an early education which enhanced his cognitive development. In short, this study shows again the importance of early pedagogical training. It does not deal with a particular school setup but can and must be done in such a way that the child can overcome his lack of social and familial stimulation. In particular, Kami, in her experience with Ypsilanti children found many favorable results by taking very young children into an extensive teaching practice. The newly created Parent Child Center in Pine Ridge would be very effective in providing this type of assistance. It is interesting to observe that it does not require much financial investment to get to the child on the one hand, and to give him fair assurance of normal behavior on the other. In mental retardation, for example, it is emphasized over and over that a diagnostic must be made as early as possible in order to be able to prevent the formation of undesirable behaviors. If today we talk more and more about pseudo-mental retardation the importance of an early diagnostic should be clear; intensive supplementary teaching procedures should be applied as soon as possible, to these 3-, 4-, and 5-year-old children.

There are naturally other types of pedagogical implications which can be molded into practical recommendations. We have insisted that one of the tragedies of teaching is the application of global procedures to what should be individualized teaching. One can well distinguish between a rate of development which is individual, and a stage of acquisition which is global. This leads us to the idea of specifying a particular time to teach one particular concept, which must be when the child is able to integrate a particular type of information. This study suggests, as did the Geneva results, that some things such as correspondences can be taught very early, because these early acquisitions are prerequisites for later fundamental acquisitions. Thus the understanding of the construction of cognitive development and its mechanisms leads us to understand what teaching procedures are possible for very young children. Later, certainly there are other ways. One such method has been described by Decroly, and consists in providing what we call centers of interest. This applies not only to work areas, but also in the provision of meaningful purpose in the study of one particular problem. For example, one can conceive of the multitude of ramifications a simple question such as studying oil production; this would lead the children not only to work together but also to obtain valuable information in terms of knowledge. If we understand well that learning is not an increase in the amount of information, but sequential organization, we can see the fruitfulness of such ideas such as centers of interest; for here the goal is decided and its fulfillment depends upon the cooperation of many and not only upon competition. The meaningful study of particular problems can be extremely helpful not only in increasing the amount of knowledge among children, but also in increasing communication between them.

Another pedagogical implication is the breakup of the grading system so that instead of competing in the classroom, children can cooperate with each other. For example, an 8-year-old child could talk with a 6-year-old in order to solve a problem which has been decided by the teacher. Thus, not only would the teacher be relieved of the problem of having so many children in a classroom, but we would see that each would help the other. One of the most important ideas is that of reciprocity. Reciprocity becomes a fact when people get together to work on a particular problem, and it is as important for children as it is for adults. In other words, groups based on reciprocal relations should be enhanced whenever possible.

There is an important point to be made concerning the attitude of the teacher. If a teacher does not believe that his children are clever, certainly the children will fulfill no more than his level of expectation. Today, we hear of such things as the "low expectation vacuum ideology;" our results strongly suggest that low expectations are a consequence of the teacher's attitude rather then of a lack of the child's cognitive abilities. Given the relatively undeveloped background in which we have conducted our study as compared with that of Geneva, and finding not only the same tendencies of cognitive functioning but also quasi-norms which are almost superimposed upon each other, we can say that there is no reason to doubt that these children are clever and that they do develop well. One of their problems, however, maybe that perhaps their teachers do not believe in them. It is important for the teacher to have faith in the child; his enthusiasm will be shared by the child. This is one very important factor in any teaching situation.

Some other practical suggestions are for older children. The introduction of unstructured lab periods, where the child can actually experiment with his knowledge rather than having it displayed only verbally to him. For example, a type of laboratory physics, dealing with simple physical facts will enhance his logico-mathematical development as well as his physical knowledge. Again, we observe that we are really enhancing not the amount of information, but the organizational framework in which the child works in order to proceed to the formal level of thinking.

Another suggestion is to de-emphasize tests and the values attached to them. Reading tests and tests such as the CAT or the Thorndyke are undoubtedly good for evaluating the child, but useless in generating realistic teaching procedures. We obtain only a result - a number. Whether the result is good or bad, it will follow the child almost all of his life. Not only are these tests unfair to the child but they are unfair to his future. One should remember that Einstein did not walk before he was five; yet he became Einstein. There are many Einstein children who do not develop because some labels have been attached to them and have affected them for the rest of their lives. It is interesting to note that IQ tests, which should be used to the advantage of the child, are usually used evaluatively rather than helping us to understand the child's capabilities. In other words, the process of how the child learns, the means of providing a school environment which enhances development is important to cognitive development itself.

Of great importance in the lack of motivation to learn is the indifference of parents in the education of their children. Lack of parental involvement in the educational system should certainly be overcome as much as possible. One way of moving toward this goal is by providing meaningful information to the parents not in terms of an evaluation of the child, but by showing them what can be done in order to help him develop in a meaningful world.

Certainly it has been shown again and again that Pine Ridge children are underachieving and dropping out of school at an alarming rate. There is no reason for this, on intellectual grounds. Those children whom we tested develop cognitively in the same way as other children; certainly it is not a lack of intelligence which is responsible for this situation. In their study on conditions among the Oglala Sioux on the Pine Ridge Reservation Dr. Eileen Maynard and Gayla Twiss [16] stress the importance of parents being involved in the education of their children. We would like to make this conclusion also ours, as well as we would like to make ours their admonishment to educators: "understand and respect your Indian students and show greater interest in their culture." It is important to note that all our results show that there is no reason to believe that Indian children underachieve because of cognitive or hereditary factors, as Jensen would like to see it [47].

In short, our pedagogical recommendations move from practical recommendations to theoretical considerations. We can see there that a deep relationship exists between cognitive development and pedagogical implications. Among Indian children it is possible to overcome many of the early difficulties encountered by the children by providing a meaningful pedagogical environment involving some very simple teaching techniques. These methods have not been used by many people, yet they have been shown to be very successful. In a recent article, published by D. Henninger and N. Esposito [48], in the New York Review of Books, the Rough Rock Demonstration School in northern Arizona is spoken of as a welcome anomaly in the chain of dead and desert schools. The curriculum at this school includes daily instruction in Navajo culture, history, and language and the school's culture identification. The same type of project could be done here, on the one hand having Indian culture respected and Indian history being taught, and on the other hand respecting fundamental concepts which are basic for understanding history and everyday life in general. We certainly approve of the Rough Rock Demonstration School, but we disapprove of the fact that it is only a demonstration school, that it is only a project. For education does not require only money. It requires that one understand the logic of development and then that one develop teaching procedures which although not expensive can be most helpful to the development of the child. The idea of emphasizing and teaching Indian culture, as done now in the Holy Rosary Mission in Pine Ridge, we can applaud. But at the same time the basic features of cognitive development should also be emphasized, for without teaching the universals, teaching history alone is not sufficient for enhancing development. The two are complementary. The modalities are simple; essentially the implementation is a practical problem.

VIII

Conclusion

THEORETICAL PART

We have provided some hypothesis that we intend to survey in our results. The first deals with the fundamental sequential process in the development of thinking which can be true or not for Oglala as compared with Geneva children. There is no question that our results show that the succession of stages is respected among both populations. If we have insisted upon the relativity of the percentages and norms within our sample and if we did not provide any statistical evidences other than scalogram or percentages, it was because we were involved in understanding the nature of the cognitive development more than in the establishment of norms. Taking this point of view we observe is a strong superimposition between the type of stages discovered in Geneva and the stages encountered among Oglala children. For instance, we have been able to show that within our nine experiments there was never more than one year of time delay between the achievement in Geneva and that among the Oglalas. Most of the time we observed that the acquisitions were made at the same age; we never observed any reversal patterns in regard to the acquisition of any particular concept or more than one year of difference. These results are important, as are the ways by which we have been able to show that some prerequisite concepts are achieved by Oglalas in the same way that they are among Geneva children. This is relevant for the process of construction of concrete operational thinking. For instance, in regard to conservation we have been able to show that the one-to-one correspondence is acquired earlier than any other form of conservation. The next to be acquired was conservation of matter followed very closely by liquid and later by weight and length. It appears that the one-to-one correspondence is a logical prerequisite for building further classifications; this is also what we have found here experimentally.

In itself finding the same succession of stages is an important result and the consequence of having dealt with a large number of logical realms rather than the study of one particular concept. We have obtained thus, a picture of cognitive development which can be completely compared with Geneva children.

That has led us to the idea of logical necessities of the cognitive development upon which we have insisted. The same holds for space: geometrical drawings are achieved earlier than are simple perspectives which implies all sorts of reconstruction at different levels. Here too, our research has been able to demonstrate a greater understanding of the true cognitive nature of spatial development which is usually seen as only of perceptual origin. But the fact that complex transformations are not achieved before the formal level of thinking strongly suggests a deep relationship between space and logico-mathematical growth.

The logic of development is respected for both samples and it is important to see that this logic stems from an internal process as well as an external one, and not from cultural factors per se.

Our second hypothesis dealing with the basic value of Piaget's approach, has been fully confirmed. Precisely in finding that Oglala children do develop in the same way that Genevan children do, we have shown its basic importance. Transitivity is for instance really inherent in the logic of the number and therefore is rather independent of any social or cultural bias. In order to deal with numbers and counting, transitivity is a prerequisite and hence is not culturally imposed. Thus, in facing the critique that Piaget's tests, are not sensible to cultural values we see why they do not seek this "sensibility." They are not meant to direct themselves toward culture. They are meant to embody fundamental underlying structures.

In regard to our third hypothesis concerning the rate of development we have observed that in many studies such as Bovet [6], Hyde [7], and Bruner [5], time delays in the acquisitions of basic concepts are found although within a respect for the order of succession of stages. We have no reason to believe that among Oglala children such is the case. No real time delays have been observed. Each concept that we have studied among Oglalas is almost contemporary with Geneva norms.

Our fourth hypothesis, dealing with the relationship between language and cognition has brought an extremely meaningful result relative to the time of acquisition of the logic of classes and of seriation. What we have found is that both are achieved almost at the same age. Since classification seems to be influenced by language

more than seriation, whereas seriation seems to be more perceptual
than classification, given the fact that the Lakota language presents
on the surface a rather weak classificatory quality (in particular
when its temporal organization is observed) we could have found
classification to be more delayed than it is the case. Reciprocally,
since seriation is a "good form" at least in the sense of the Gestalt
we should have found that seriation is achieved much earlier. We
found neither of these results. The reason lies in the fact that
seriation does not derive from strictly perceptual features and
classification does not stem from verbal structures. Both derive from
the general sensorimotor coordination; their origins are in the
actions and their subsequent organization. In finding this contemporary construction we have been able to display a confirmation of
Piaget's point of view concerning the common origin of seriation and
classification. This is in itself an important fact and it leads
again to the recognition of the importance of early active functional
exercises as we have stressed in the pedagogical recommendations. No
doubt some kind of language ability is essential for the completion
of such structures as classification but it is essentially because
operations involve a symbolic and therefore a representative handling
of objects that they go beyond what could be done in terms of overt
behaviors. But again we insist that language alone is not enough.
This means that sensorimotor and perceptual factors combine to give
to the primitive figural collections their positive features. In
other words seriation is also the results not only of a perceptual
construction of "good form" but even more the result of a process of
active organization that the child provides from the sensorimotor to
the concrete operational period of thinking.

Our fifth hypothesis deals with learning. Our results have
strongly shown that a deep relationship exists between a learning
modality and the cognitive stage at which the child functions. For
instance the purely pre-operational child in space is not going to
integrate anything more than local positions and may eventually
achieve a correct result through a local type of strategy. Therefore
we will speak of learning in terms of levels of organization in the
same sense as Piaget speaks of sequential equilibrium rather than of
learning as particular and specific features to be introduced in the
course of cognitive development.

This is an important difference - one which stresses the sequential organizational patterns rather than specific means to lean. It
leads us to a recognition of the reliability of some pedagogical procedures such as Montessori, Decroly, or Kami. Learning is related to
the cognitive stage in the sense that it represents organizational
patterns which can be enhanced in order to favor the development of
the underlying structure. The fact that we have been able to show
that this is also true for Oglala children constitutes a result in
itself. This correlation between a modality of learning and a stage
of development is not surprising as soon as we recall the progressive
organization and equilibration that Piaget constantly emphasizes.

In a recent article by Inhelder, Bovet, and Sinclair three problems are raised in regard to learning.

1   The role of the factors contributing to the genesis of logical structures. In our study we have seen that even if language or perception are important, the most crucial factor is the nature of the relationship among those factors.

2   In regard to the nature of this relationship: we have been able to show that clear operational sub-systems exist which are consistent with a functional continuity as well as a structural discontinuity. The modalities of learning will also be consistent with a particular sub-system: e.g. local learning when the child is pre-operational this leads to a better understanding of the organizational pattern of development.

3   The temporal aspect of this organizational process is also important. Our results have shown the nature of this order of succession and thus the hierarchy of subsequent structures. For example, if the one-to-one correspondence is a prerequisite for the construction of elementary logic then a teaching procedure should enhance this type of temporal organization.

When in one of our recent articles [49] we emphasized that one of the major aims in education was to create an openness to cognitive contradictions what we see here too is that this openness is not a random one but follows a logic which is intrinsic to the logic of cognitive development. In other words it is not randomly that the child can integrate cognitive contradictions but that cognitive contradictions become meaningful as soon as his cognitive structure allows it to do so.

What we have seen too is that we cannot divorce specific achievements for a particular concept from this the general system of thinking which constitutes the concrete operational period of thinking. Stressed also in our results is the generality of such concepts as true reversibility which is implied in the understanding of almost all our situations Piaget insists upon the distinction between empirical reversibility and true reversibility, with only the latter being characteristic of concrete thinking; our results reveal how fruitful this distinction is. The generality of reversible thinking which does not stem from an argument of identity, as Bruner would like to believe, is here also clearly stressed.

But let us recall the different factors which are usually voiced in order to explain development. One of these is maturation. Maturation however is not sufficient because none of the dynamic structures are innate; they form very gradually. Our research with Oglala children has shown this gradual formation of those operatory structures. This progressive construction does not seem to depend primarily upon maturation because we observe among Oglala children too that the achievements hardly corresponds to a particular age. What we have found is that only the order of succession is constant. Certainly again one cannot deny the crucial role that maturation plays but this role is determined above all by existing possibilities. There exists a distance between a potentiality and its actualization. In short the factors of innateness seem above all limited; neither Oglala nor Geneva children have an intuition of conservation or space; they build it.

Factors concerning physical experiences are certainly important too. Experiences with objects play a very important role in the establishment of dynamic structures because operations originate from actions. But its role manifests itself right at the beginning of sensorimotor explorations which precede language and it affirms itself continually in the course of manipulation and activities which are appropriate in seeking the progressive changes.

But as Piaget points out [50] (p.278), as necessary as the role of experience may be it is not sufficient to describe the construction of these dynamic structures for three reasons at least.

1   There are ideas which cannot possibly be derived from experience alone. For instance conservation, which is not taught as such in school, is nevertheless achieved by the children. And even if one would try to teach it, one would clearly observe that it cannot be done as such. Conservation is the product of a dynamic deduction and not part of an experience. It is a true discovery of the child.

2   All the results dealing with the learning of logical structures show that one does not learn it as one can learn a physical law. The logical structures always suppose a coordinating activity of the subject although meaningful teaching may enhance it.

     But there exist two types of experiences: (a) the physical experiences show the object as it is; and this leads to a direct abstraction from the object (b) the logico-mathematical experiences which refer to the result of the actions rather than to the objects themselves. Logico-mathematical knowledge does not stem from the same type of learning as the physical experiences do. Thus, the importance of a point of view of successive equilibration rather than that of additive knowledge becomes apparent.

3   Relative to social interaction we can see that the educative and social transmissions naturally play an important role in the formation of dynamic structures. But they are not sufficient either. First, a certain number of structures do not lend themselves to teaching and are prior to all teaching. Second, many discoveries that the child makes during his life are not due to educative or social transmissions.

For instance, in order to understand the adult and his language the child needs the means of assimilation and accommodation which exist before the social transmission itself and as a matter of fact prepares it.

All the previous factors are extremely crucial. We observe thus that all exchanges between the organism and the milieu are composed of two poles; one dealing with the assimilation of the given external to some internal structures, the other dealing with the accommodation of the structures to the already present ones. The result is an equilibration between the assimilation and the accommodation.

In summary our research has brought new results in many ways: the general superimposition of the sequential aspect of cognitive development itself among Oglala and Geneva children; the relations between a modality of learning and the cognitive stage; the different aspects of spatial relations dealing with simple or complex relations as related to a concrete or a formal level of thinking; the relevance of organizational factors internal to the logic of the child is creating the conditions which make him permeable to cognitive contradictions; and above all the importance of an equilibrationist's point of view rather than one which sees development in terms of an increase of knowledge.

But some questions still remain open, such as all those dealing with the real mechanism of this equilibration. In this sense the real question of learning remain open, namely, what are the real sequences of organizational learning. Its understanding will lead to a real resolution of the problems of learning which we are still far from being able to understand.

IX

A Plea for the Indians and Indianness

Vine Deloria, Jr., in a recent publication [51] (p.100), says in talking about anthropologists,

"I would expect an instantaneous rebuttal by the "knowledgable" anthros that these sentiments do not "represent" all the Indians. They don't today. They will tomorrow. In the meantime it would be wise for anthropologists to get down from their thrones of authority and pure research and begin helping Indian tribes instead of preying on them. For the wheel of Karma grinds slowly but it does grind finely. And it makes a complete circle."

It is true that research must be done in order to come to any valid conclusions about cognitive development. On the other hand, it may very well be the case that we as psychologists and anthropologists have not relinquished our thrones of authority. However, what we have been trying to do is to begin to show how Indian children develop and to help provide some meaningful ways of implementing new pedagogical techniques based on this approach. This is the meaning of a new day which might come, a day when educational purposes will be meaningful and when relevant education will be provided for all children. In accomplishing this, one can cite the work of Father Bryde, S.J., author of "Modern Indian Psychology" [52], as providing tools for education in terms of Indian values. But, in order to successfully deal with Indian values and Indian children in the context of the larger world, one must also understand what is common to all children. That which is common to all children seems more and more to be the logical operations of cognitive development which do not appear to be culturally based, but which develop according to an

136

internal order which transcends culture. We have, in our research, focused not upon those superficial products of cognitive development usually measured by standard IQ tests, but rather upon deep structures, stages of cognitive development which constitute the developmental capacity for intellectual functioning, and hence achievement. These deep structures must be proven again and again to be independent of a given culture.

For in each culture there must exist a type of trade-off between teaching historical values and discovering viable ways in which people can develop their own abilities. Logic has the virtue of being independent of the social milieu through which it is expressed. In other words, logic derives from the very roots of the rules that objects appear to follow in their behavior toward each other and the way in which we internalize them. This is Piaget's point about the internal necessity of sequential cognitive development rather than dependence upon a cultural pattern. Our results tend to confirm this point. In fact, we have done three things in our research: the first was to assess the development of cognition among Indian children. Moreover, through the many discussions which were held with teachers, parents, and people involved in the education of children on the reservation, we have been able to understand some of the educational problems which are posed here. Finally, we have been able to suggest what may be some very meaningful ways in which to enhance the development of young children through education.

One important thing which may have come out of these investigations is the fact that one can distinguish two separate realms in teaching. One is the realm of history, i.e., that in which the cultural values are strongly implicated. The other realm, is independent of the cultural background and implies the following of similar paths by all children in the development of a system of understanding reality. When, in our introduction we insisted upon the presence of logical necessities, we were trying to focus upon these logical necessities internal to the process of cognitive development.

In a recent work by A. Schorr [53] (p.166), we can read the following in the conclusion:

"Sixteen million poor children are 16 million too many.
Whatever our problems - and we have them to work out - we
have the resources to see that no child in the United
States is poor. We are rich enough to wipe out poverty of
the nineteenth-century variety: rats, rags, and rickets.
We can now complete the task. Because our standard of
living is rising so rapidly we are in a position - without
perceptible cost to any individual - to wipe out poverty of
the twentieth-century variety: evidenced when any child has
dramatically less of life's goods than the average child
has."

Schorr is certainly right in his argument. But we want to insist upon the fact that it does not necessarily cost more money to provide a meaningful education. What it costs is enthusiasm and belief on the part of the teacher, a knowledge that the situation of the Indian child is temporary. It can be solved through meaningful educational resources. Our research has been able to show that there is not one reason to believe that the Indian child is in any sense of the word, backward, or behind his American or European white peer in terms of intellectual functioning.

In our results, we can see the beginning of a decline in performance around the age of 10. This strongly suggests that the problem is not only a cognitive one. We wish to stress the fact that it is around this age that a large cluster of transformations in the process of thinking do occur, which Piaget has called the development of the formal level of thinking. We have conducted no systematic research with children who have reached or passed the stage of the development of this formal level of thinking as time did not permit inclusion of this group in the sample, but we know that around 9-10 the child begins to realize gradually what his social position is. If around 16-17 we observe among Oglala children on the reservation a great number of dropouts greater than in many other parts of the United States, then we must ask ourselves if the problem involved is not primarily a socio-economic one rather than an intellectual one. Our research strongly suggests that there is not one cognitive reason that these children should not achieve a normal integration into society. Rather, they have all the cognitive skills to do so. The problem then among Oglala children seems to be socio-economically based. For if we can find basically the same sequence of developmental stages as was observed among White American and Swiss children, then we have every reason to believe that there are other features in the situation which account for the later dropouts which we observe among adolescents.

In their Baseline Data Study, Dr Eileen Maynard and Mrs Gayla Twiss conclude that jobs and industries should be integrated into the Pine Ridge community to alleviate the employment problem on the reservation. Certainly it is a waste of human nature to encourage children to develop in a normal way and arrive at the stage where they fully realize their social position yet give them no way of surpassing it. On the other hand, many Indians say they would like to remain on the reservation because they are among their people; it is good that this Indian identification is strong; but the reservation socio-economic structure does not provide them with the possibilities of achieving a meaningful life. This is a scandal; another scandal is the lack of humanity manifested by those whose interests lie in not seeing anything growing from within the reservation.

It is important to know too, that the Oglala children who develop normally in comparison with their Geneva peers do not have the

same opportunities as others in terms of education and later socio-
economic participation, and that in itself is a scandal. It is a
waste of human resources, a dwarfing human potential. It is a waste
for the economy, and it is a direct appeal to children not to develop
participation in their world. It is not respecting the individual
person, his development, his historical background to not provide him
with everything. It is not respecting the Indian in his own historical Indianness to force him to under employment, and that is what is
being done with these children. One can well emphasize their education. One can well give them more or different "teaching procedures." One can well do all sorts of things to enhance their educational standard. But if all three factors, social, economic, and
psychological are not taken into account together, and faced
together, then there are no real possibilities to completely solve
the problems.

If we observe that the median family income is $1500 for
Indians, whereas in the general population it is $6682; that the
unemployment rate is 45% for Indians vs 4.6% for the general population; if the average schooling for adults is five years for Indians
and 11.7 years for the general population; if the average life ex-
pectancy is 63.5 years for Indians and 70.2 years for the general
population, if the infant mortality rate is 38.9 for the Indian and
24.8 for the general population; if the incidence of tuberculosis per
100 population is 184 among Indians vs 26.6 for the general population; if the average school dropout rate is 50% among Indians and
29% for the general population; if the birthrate is 43.1 among the
Indians and 21.0 among the general population, then the problem of
underachievement is not purely a psychological one, and other factors
are involved   (Source, Education Age, April, 1967).

Moreover, again and again these Indian children have been tested
using nationwide standardized tests for comparison such as that of
Fall, 1965   (Source: Equality of Educational Opportunity OE 38001,
Table 9).

This is another example of ethnocentrism used to the detriment
of the Indian. What we have tried to do in our study, is to discover
a non-culturally biased way of assessing the cognitive development of
the Indians. Moreover, with this method of approach we discover that
the Indian develops completely normally, and that there is no functional reason for him to be behind in achievement. If they test below
average, it is because of the tools that have been used in order to
test them; it is not because of a lack of intelligence, but rather
because of a lack of the perceived possibility of living a meaningful
life.   Again, one can construct a picture of the great verbal lag
between White-rural southwest and Indian children as compared with
students living in the northeastern United States, and we can discover that at the sixth grade the Indians are 1.7 years behind, and
for the ninth grade 2.1 years behind and at the twelfth grade 3.5

years behind in verbal performance. Relative to mathematical functioning one can observe that the Indians are 2.0 years behind at the
sixth grade, 2.4 years behind at the ninth grade, and 3.9 years
behind at the twelfth grade   (Source: Equality of Educational Opportunity OE 38001, Tables 3.121.1 and 3.121.3).

If this lag increases, it is not because of a lack of innate
intelligence but rather because of a deepening sense of hopelessness
due to the perceived lack of social and economic possibilities. There
is no functional reason why the Indian should be behind and taken as
a second-rate subject.

In a recent monograph,   Murray and Wax [19], begin the last
chapter, Summary and Recommendations, with a statement of the
theories by which their research was born:

Theory 1   Cultural disharmony. To children reared in conservative
             Indian fashion, the atmosphere of a normal American
             school is painful, incomprehensible and even immoral.
             But, to teachers of (normal) lower middle class American
             backgrounds, the behavior of the students is open un-
             disciplined, lacking in scholastic initiative and even
             immoral.

Theory 2   Lack of Motive Unappealing Curricula. The notions of the
             Indian people themselves as to careers that are possible
             and desirable are somewhat much at variance with those of
             the educators. Where this variance exists, dropout of
             adolescent students is exceedingly likely.

Theory 3   Preservation of Identity. To conservative Indians, their
             identity as Indians is the last and most valuable
             treasure remaining to them. Insofar as education is
             presented to them, or perceived by them, as a technique
             for transmuting their children and their people into
             "Whites," then it becomes freighted with all manner of
             emotional complications and is likely to be rejected.
             (p. 112).

Their findings, and ours, particularly concerning the second
theory, partially confirm these expectations. In particular, Indian
parents and their children usually see education as a potential key
to vocational success. But the difficulty again is that since little
employment is available on or near the reservation, where most Sioux
prefer to dwell, then the problem is not an intellectual one but an
economic one. Education becomes irrelevant to the reservation opportunity structure. Concerning their first theory, cultural disharmony,
if a school is painful, then it is destructive to the Indianness
that they should seek to enhance. We have already distinguished
between two foci in education: the focus on the cognitive realm and

the other, the focus on the realm of old values. The necessary synthesis can be accomplished through meaningful education where the school becomes the vehicle to carry both and not simply a confined place to perform irrelevant tasks.

In his statement to the Senate Committee on Indian Education, Karl Mindell [54], former director of the Pine Ridge Community Mental Health Program, strongly emphasizes, the relation between psychological and socio-economical factors. He says,

"To look briefly at some specific mental health programs, and possible mental health problems, we will note that the suicide attempt rate is more than twice the national average, that the delinquency rate for children between 10 and 17 is almost nine times the national overall average, that problems with the use of alcohol are extensive, that many pubertal children sniff gasoline for its intoxicating effects, that almost one in every five adolescents have no adult man in their family, that the number of children in foster homes here is almost five times the national rate." (p.3).

and he continues by emphasizing that most of the problems mentioned above are not secondary to Indian-White differences, but are secondary to other circumstances such as socio-economic ones. He ends by saying that our job is to help the Indian develop his strength. A strength that makes middle-class White America look (socially) deprived in comparison; their interest in people rather than things, their strong feeling of belonging, and of a need to share with others a sense of dignity in harsh circumstances, and their measuring of love not by what one has or looks like or says but by what he is.

In this particular sense our research did show that all Indians have the cognitive abilities to assure the development of those particular strengths. But as long as the situation remains economically deprived there is little hope; as long as better education is not inserted into a meaningful socio-economic milieu, it cannot have the results that we should be able to expect with relevant teaching procedures.

In "The Last Days of the Sioux Nation" [55] Utley observes, when speaking of Wounded Knee, "the Sioux suffered two conquests: a military conquest and a psychological conquest. It was the latter which destroyed them as a nation and left emotional scars that persist today, but the road that ended in the second conquest began before the first; it began in the old life."

Yet there is another psychological conquest which the Indian can make himself. It is this conquest which will enhance his Indianness and those values which Mindell speaks of, which would make middle-class White America look culturally deprived. It is the synthesis between a meaningful cognitive development and an integration of Indian values which will finally decide if the psychological conquest that the Indian lived through around 1890, will remain only a regression in the service of a further development. For, it is a well-known fact that regression can have many facets. But one this regression is overcome, and the dependency upon the White man is surpassed, then a synthesis which will be Indian in its own values is going to be achieved. It is important to begin it at the beginning of life, at the beginning of the educational process. It is important to carry it through toward an integration in the twentieth century. There is no cut and dried solution for that. But certainly the Indian child is well equipped to be able to face such a psychological conquest, and this means that the price which has been paid is a price not only towards the rebirth of the Indian identity, but more a price towards the development taking into account this Indian synthesis that only Indians will be doing.

It is important to note that the Indian possesses all the capabilities to attain normal functioning, but as long as he submits to surveys which are unfair to his culture, to tests which do not lead to an understanding of what he really is, the situation is not going to change. Certainly IQ tests have been widely used, however, if all IQ tests would be based on Indian Winter Counts rather than White values, we would see Whites appearing extremely unfavorably. There is no IQ test for values which are Indian. There are no tests to assess an interest in people rather than things. There are no tests to assess a strong feeling of belonging, of identity, of a need to share with other; yet these are the type of "tests" for which the Indians are best suited. Piaget [20] and Kohlberg [21] for example, have shown that the last stage of moral development is one of reciprocity, and it is of great importance to know that the Indian realized this a long time ago.

"That these people may live" is the closing line title of Maynard and Twiss's study. In conclusion, this is what we would like to see. That these people may live, that they may have the opportunities to build a meaningful life according to their Indian identity.

Part II

Part II

X

The Individual Reports

In order to facilitate the reading as well as the understanding of the individual reports and in order to protect as much as possible the anonymity of each subject we have proceeded in the following way:

I GENERAL CONSIDERATIONS

1. All the subjects have been grouped according to their age. Each age group is a complete year. In other words, we did not classify our subject according to their school grades. Thus, we divide our sample in 7 groups ranging from age 4 to 10.

2. Each subject has been assigned a number. The first refers to his age in terms of year the last digit refers to his position within his age group. The second number refers to his position within our global sample. Thus subject 405/5 is actually a 4-year-old child, is number five in his age group and number 5 in our total sample.

II CHART I

A first chart (Chart I) provides the following information: the name, the number, the age, the different experiments passed, their total, the sex and the school where the child came from. We grouped our experiment according to their logical meaning: the first group concerns conservation which contains five experiments: conservation of matter, liquid, length, weight, and the one-to-one correspondence (1:1). The second group concerns the spatial relationship with two experiments: perspectives (Mountain) and geometrical drawings. The

145

Chart I

List of Subjects with Number Qualified as observation no.: + too poor

m = mainstream
— = Common
PR = Pine Ridge Resk
♀ = girls ♂ = boys

Sex	Sch. Ages 4-5	Age at testing (months)	Obs. No.	Conservation						Spon		El. Exp.		P. L.
				Matter	Liquid	Length	Weight	no. 1	Number	Donor	Problem	Solution	Conclu.
♂ m.	1. Billy McLaughlin	4;0	401/1	✓	✓	✓	0	✓	0	✓	✓	✓	0
♀ L.	2. Roxie Ann Dreamer	4;0	402/2	✓	✓	✓	0	✓	0	✓	0	✓	0
♂ m.	3. Joey Yankton	4;3	403/3	✓	✓	0	0	✓	0	✓	0	✓	0
♀ L.	4. Marie Makes Room Rose	4;3	404/4	✓	✓	✓	0	✓	0	✓	0	✓	0
♂ L.	5. Darren Bad Heart Bull	4;4	405/5	✓	0	✓	0	✓	0	✓	0	✓	0
♀ m.	6. Lisa Steele	4;6	406/6	✓	✓	✓	0	✓	0	✓	✓	✓	0
♀ L.	7. Justina Gross	4;6	407/7	✓	✓	✓	0	✓	0	✓	0	✓	0
♀ L.	8. Pauline Two Bulls	4;7	408/8	0	✓	✓	0	✓	0	✓	0	✓	0
♂ m.	9. Seelo Bissonette Jr.	4;11	409/9	✓	✓	✓	0	✓	0	✓	✓	✓	0
♂ m.	10. Theodore Blackbird	4;11	410/10	✓	✓	✓	0	✓	0	✓	✓	✓	0
50% 5M 5♀ 6♂			N= 10	9	8	9	0	10	0	10	6	10	0
50% 5L													
0%	Ages: 5-6												
♀ m.	11. Rose Stoulieu	5;0	501/11	✓	✓	✓	0	✓	0	✓	0	✓	0
♂ PR.	12. Gilbert Long	5;1	502/12	✓	✓	✓	0	✓	✓	✓	✓	✓	0
♂ m.	13. Wayne Sleeping Bear	5;2	503/13	✓	✓	✓	0	✓	0	✓	✓	✓	0
♂ PR.	14. Michael Twiss	5;2	504/14	✓	✓	✓	0	✓	0	✓	✓	✓	0
♀ m.	15. Kathy McLaughlin	5;2	505/15	✓	✓	✓	0	✓	0	✓	0	✓	0
♀ L.	16. Antony Crazy Thunder	5;3	506/16	✓	0	✓	0	✓	0	✓	0	✓	0
♀ m.	17. Elizabeth Buffington	5;4	507/17	✓	✓	✓	0	✓	0	✓	✓	✓	0
♂ L.	18. Janice Iron Dog	5;5	508/18	✓	✓	✓	0	✓	0	✓	0	✓	0
♀ PR.	19. Jody Twiss	5;6	509/19	✓	✓	✓	0	✓	0	✓	0	✓	0
♂ L.	20. Robin Bad Heart Bull	5;7	510/20	✓	✓	✓	0	✓	0	✓	0	✓	✓
40% 4M 4♀ 6♂			N= 10	9	8	10	0	10	4	10	7	10	0
30% 4L													
30% 3PR	Ages: 6-7												
♀ PR.	21. Connie Morgan	6;1	601/21	✓	✓	✓	0	✓	✓	✓	✓	0	0
♀ PR.	22. Shawn Kirk	6;3	602/22	✓	✓	✓	0	✓	✓	0	✓	✓	0
♀ PR.	23. Clay Twiss	6;4	603/23	✓	✓	0	0	✓	✓	0	✓	✓	0
♂ PR.	24. Francis Fay	6;6	604/24	✓	✓	✓	✓	✓	0	✓	0	✓	0
♀ PR.	25. Joyce Reynolds	6;8	605/25	✓	0	0	0	✓	0	✓	0	✓	0
♀ PR.	26. Evelyn Tail	6;8	606/26	✓	✓	✓	0	✓	0	✓	0	✓	0
♀ PR.	27. Dorothy Tyon	6;9	607/27	✓	✓	✓	0	✓	✓	0	✓	✓	0
♂ m.	28. Michael Bissonette	6;10	608/28	0	✓	✓	0	✓	0	0	0	✓	0
♀ PR.	29. Sheldon Eagle Elk	6;11	609/29	✓	✓	✓	0	0	0	✓	✓	✓	0
♂ L.	30. David Clifford	6;11	610/30	✓	✓	✓	✓	✓	0	✓	0	✓	0
10% 1M 7♀ 3♂			N= 10	10	10	8	2	10	4	8	10	0	
10% 1L													
30% 8PR 7♀ 3♂			N=10										

List of Subjects with Number
qualified to observations no.
+ loco primi

Schools Age: 10-11	Age	No.	Conservations					Space		El. Logic		F. L
	Yrs + month		Matter	Liquid	Length	Weight	1:1	Horiz.	Quant.	Inclus.	Disjunc.	implication
L 42. Dolores Eagle Hawk	10;0	100/42	✓	✓	✓	✓	0	✓	0	✓	✓	7
m 62. Ambrose New Holy	10;1	101/62	✓	✓	✓	0	✓	✓	0	✓	✓	7
L 63. Iris Long	10;5	102/63	✓	✓	✓	✓	0	✓	0	✓	✓	7
L 64. Juanita Adams	10;7	103/64	✓	✓	✓	✓	0	✓	0	✓	✓	7
L 65. Patty Gore	10;8	104/65	✓	✓	✓	✓	0	✓	0	✓	✓	7
L 66. Roxanna Two Bulls	10;9	105/66	✓	✓	✓	✓	0	✓	0	✓	✓	7
L 67. Erletta Lamont	10;9	106/67	✓	•	✓	✓	0	✓	0	✓	✓	7
L 68. Michael White Bear Claws	10;9	107/68	✓	✓	✓	✓	0	✓	0	✓	✓	7
L 69. Christian Gross	10;9	108/69	✓	✓	✓	✓	0	✓	0	✓	✓	7
L 70. Carroll Bad Heart Bull	10;10	109/70	✓	✓	✓	✓	0	✓	0	✓	✓	7
L 71. Pearl Stewart	10;?	110/71	✓	✓	✓	✓	0	✓	✓	✓	✓	7

1 H   7 ♀   4 ♂   N=11   11   4   11   10   1/44   11   0   11   11/32   77
10 L

33 ♀   32 ♂   Total   63   67   66   50   34/265   54   32/73   61   71   1/133   472
54   46

Special cases:

♀ 0 72. Red Wing Donna	6;3	A/72	✓	0	✓	0	0	0	✓	✓	✓	5
♀ L 73. Hesitime Red Paint	9;4	A/73	✓	✓	✓	0	✓	✓	0	✓	7
♀ L 74. Ruby Belt	9;8	A/74	✓	✓	✓	0	✓	✓	✓	✓	8
♀ L 75. Connie Weasel Bear	12;8	A/75	✓	✓	✓	0	0	✓	0	✓	6

H = 18   26 %
L = 38   53
PR = 15   21
       71

Total Average No of Exp. by child   6,5
Conservation   3,7
Space   1,0
E. Logic   1,8

third group concerns elementary logic with two experiments: class-
inclusion (Inclusion) and seriation. The last group concerns formal
logic with only one experiment: combination which was passed by only
one very advanced child (708/38).

Each school is designated by a letter: (L) Loneman Day School,
(M) Manderson, and (PR) Pine Ridge Public School. Examination of the
chart will reveal for each age how many children passed each exper-
ment, each group of them, and how many in total.

Moreover, for each age one will finally find the total number of
experiments taken. Four additional children constituted special cases
and are numbered from A/72 to A/75.

III CHART II

A second chart (Chart II) provides data of the individual performances organized in the same manner as Chart I. Only the number
rather than the name is given. This second chart can serve as a
quick evaluation for each individual performance in the sense that
for each experiment the cognitive stage is indicated. In short,
level 1, concerns the most primitive behaviors, level 2 refers to the
intermediary ones, level 3 to the most elaborate ones. For some
experiments there exist sub-stages such as 2a or 2b. In this case 2a
is the most primitive behaviors within level 2, 2b the more advanced
ones.

In space, the mountain test (perspectives) has two levels indicated. This comes from the fact that we were dealing with two types
of transformations: first, simple relations, and second, complex ones.
We indicated also the type of leaning provided by the child in space
for both transformations (P1P3: simple) (P2P4: complex) and in seriation. (N) means no learning shown; (L) local learning; (M) more than
one position at a time; and (NL) generalized or no learning needed.
For further information the reader may consult the report itself, in
particular the results for each experiment.

A last column indicates the total number of experiments that
each child took. Sex is indicated in each case by the symbol to the
left of the child's number.

Each of them essentially focus the cognitive development and the
performance observed during the session. In order to facilitate this
reading we will provide some quick functional definitions:

(0) Compensation: a logical argument spontaneously used by the child
    to justify his belief in conservation. This argument refers to
    his ability to compose different parameters of the situation
    that compensate each other.

Chart II

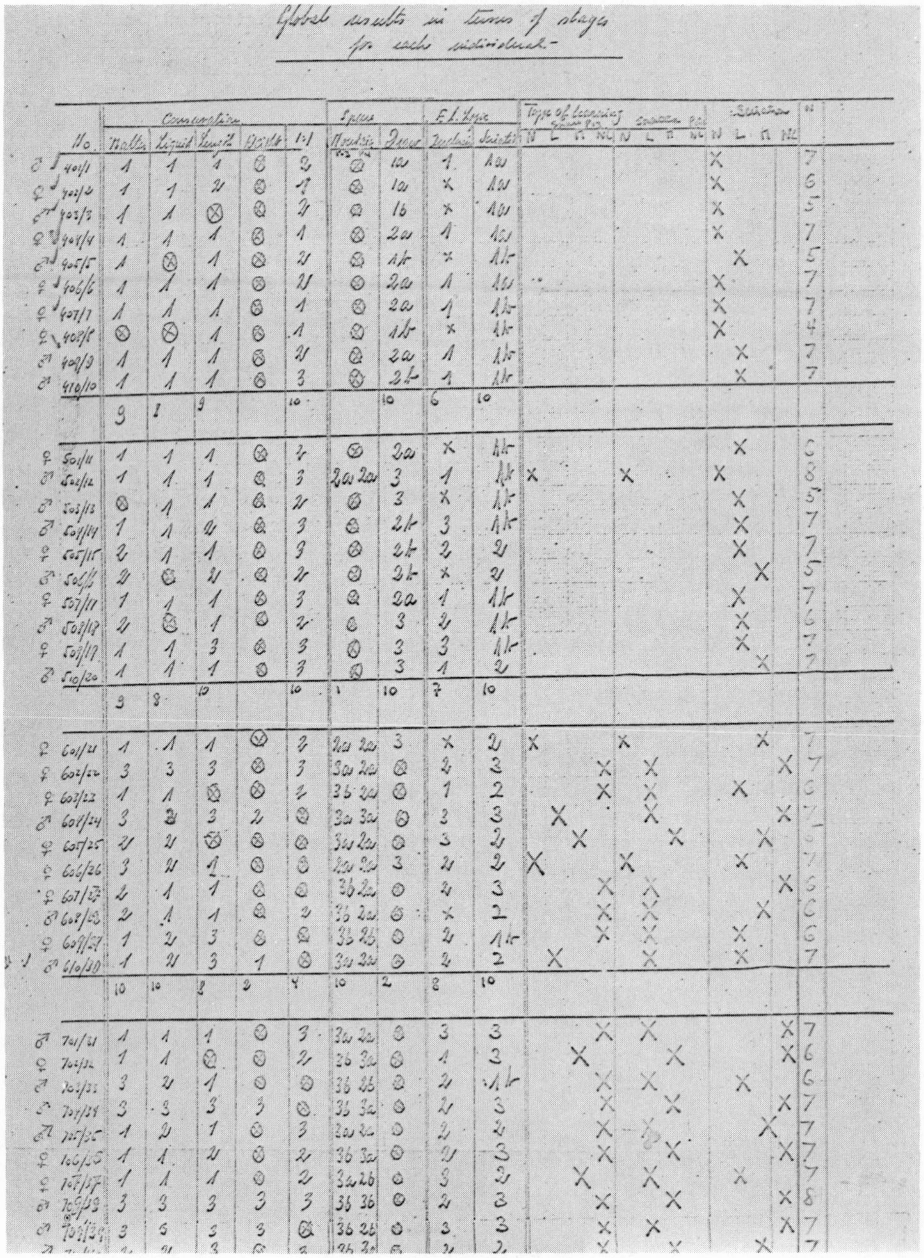

Global results in terms of stages for each individual.

No.	Conservation					Space		E.L. Logic		Type of learning (group P.O.)				(second P.O.)				Selection				N
	Matter	Liquid	Length	Weight	1:1	Horizontal	Draw	Inclusion	Seriation	N	L	R	NL	N	L	R	NL	N	L	R	NL	
♂ 401/1	1	1	1	⊗	2	⊗	1a	1	1a									X				7
♀ 402/2	1	1	2	⊗	1	⊗	1a	x	1a									X				6
♂ 403/3	1	1	⊗	⊗	2	⊗	1b	x	1a									X				5
♀ 404/4	1	1	1	⊗	1	⊗	2a	1	1a									X				7
♂ 405/5	1	⊗	1	⊗	2	⊗	1b	x	1b										X			5
♀ 406/6	1	1	1	⊗	2	⊗	2a	1	1a									X				7
♀ 407/7	1	1	1	⊗	1	⊗	2a	1	1b									X				7
♀ 408/8	⊗	⊗	1	⊗	1	⊗	1b	x	1b									X				4
♂ 409/9	1	1	1	⊗	2	⊗	2a	1	1b										X			7
♂ 410/10	1	1	1	⊗	3	⊗	2b	1	1b										X			7
	9	1	9		10		10	6	10													
♀ 501/11	1	1	1	⊗	2	⊗	2a	x	1b										X			6
♂ 502/12	1	1	1	⊗	3	2a 2a	3	1	1b	X				X				X				8
♂ 503/13	⊗	1	1	⊗	2	⊗	3	x	1b										X			5
♂ 504/14	1	1	2	⊗	3	⊗	2b	3	1b										X			7
♀ 505/15	2	1	1	⊗	3	⊗	2b	2	2										X			7
♂ 506/16	2	⊗	2	⊗	2	⊗	2b	x	2											X		5
♀ 507/17	1	1	1	⊗	3	⊗	2a	1	1b										X			7
♂ 508/18	2	⊗	1	⊗	2	⊗	3	2	1b										X			6
♀ 509/19	1	1	3	⊗	3	⊗	3	3	1b										X			7
♂ 510/20	1	1	1	⊗	3	⊗	3	1	2											X		7
	9	8	10		10	1	10	7	10													
♀ 601/21	1	1	1	⊗	2	2a 2a	3	x	2	X				X						X		7
♀ 602/22	3	3	3	⊗	3	3a 2a	⊗	2	3				X		X						X	7
♀ 603/23	1	1	⊗	⊗	2	3b 2a	⊗	1	2				X		X				X			6
♂ 604/24	3	2	3	2	⊗	3a 3a	⊗	3	3		X				X						X	7
♀ 605/25	2	2	⊗	⊗	⊗	3a 2a	⊗	3	2			X				X				X		7
♀ 606/26	3	2	1	⊗	⊗	2a 2a	3	2	2	X				X					X			7
♀ 607/27	2	1	1	⊗	⊗	3b 2a	⊗	2	3				X		X						X	6
♂ 608/28	2	1	1	⊗	2	3b 2a	⊗	x	2				X		X					X		6
♀ 609/29	1	2	3	⊗	⊗	3b 2b	⊗	2	1b				X		X				X			6
♂ 610/30	1	2	3	1	⊗	3a 2a	⊗	2	2		X				X				X			7
	10	10	8	2	4	10	2	8	10													
♂ 701/31	1	1	1	⊗	3	3a 2a	⊗	3	3				X		X						X	7
♀ 702/32	1	1	⊗	⊗	2	2b 3a	⊗	1	3			X				X					X	6
♂ 703/33	3	2	1	⊗	⊗	3b 2b	⊗	2	1b				X		X				X			6
♂ 704/34	3	3	3	3	⊗	3b 3a	⊗	2	3				X			X					X	7
♂ 705/35	1	2	1	⊗	3	2a 2a	⊗	2	2				X		X					X		7
♀ 706/36	1	1	2	⊗	2	3b 3a	⊗	2	3				X			X					X	7
♀ 707/37	1	1	1	⊗	2	3a 2b	⊗	3	2			X			X				X			7
♂ 708/38	3	3	3	3	3	3b 3b	⊗	2	3				X			X					X	8
♂ 709/39	3	3	3	3	⊗	3b 2b	⊗	3	3				X		X						X	7
♂ [illegible]	2	2	3	⊗	3	3b 3a	⊗	2	2				X			X				X		7

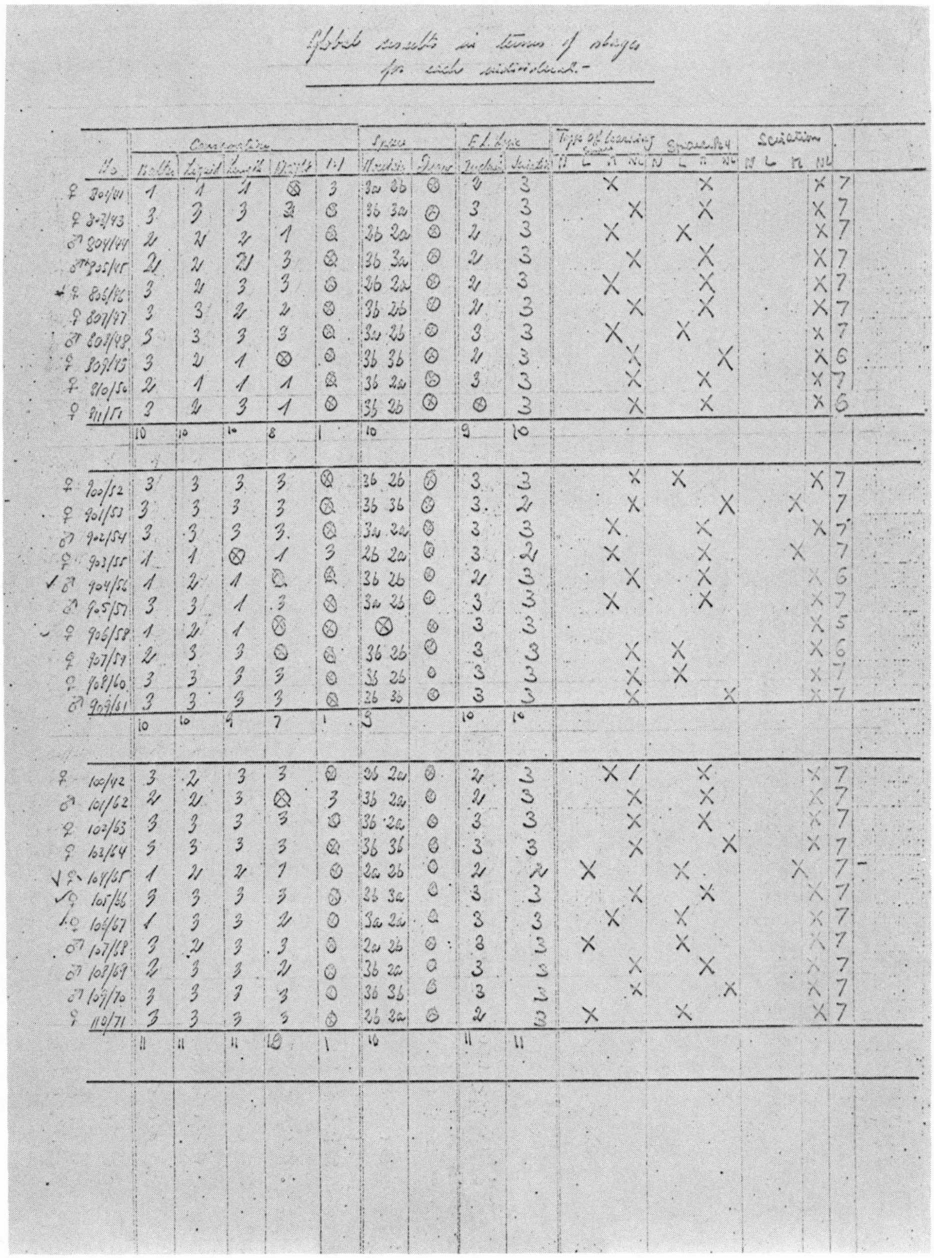

Global results in terms of stages for each individual.-

No.	Conservation					Space		E.L. type		Type of learning				Spontaneity				Seriation				
	Matter	Liquid	Length	Weight	1:1	Vertical	Decrease	Inclus.	Seriat.	N	L	R	NL	N	L	R	NL	N	L	R	NL	
♀ 801/41	1	1	1	⊗	3	3a 3b	⊗	2	3			X				X					X	7
♀ 803/43	3	3	3	3	⊗	3b 3a	⊗	3	3				X			X					X	7
♂ 804/44	2	2	2	1	⊗	2b 2a	⊗	2	3			X			X						X	7
♂ 805/45	2	2	21	3	⊗	3b 3a	⊗	2	3				X			X					X	7
+ ♀ 806/46	3	2	3	3	⊗	2b 2a	⊗	2	3			X				X					X	7
♀ 807/47	3	3	2	2	⊗	3b 2b	⊗	2	3				X			X					X	7
♂ 808/48	3	3	3	3	⊗	3a 2b	⊗	3	3			X			X						X	7
♀ 809/49	3	2	1	⊗	⊗	3b 3b	⊗	2	3				X				X				X	6
♀ 810/50	2	1	1	1	⊗	3b 2a	⊗	3	3				X			X					X	7
♀ 811/51	3	2	3	1	⊗	3b 2b	⊗	⊗	3				X			X					X	6
	10	10	10	8	1	10		9	10													
♀ 900/52	3	3	3	3	⊗	3b 2b	⊗	3	3				X		X						X	7
♀ 901/53	3	3	3	3	⊗	3b 3b	⊗	3.	2				X				X			X		7
♂ 902/54	3	3	3	3.	⊗	3a 2a	⊗	3	3			X				X					X	7
♀ 903/55	1	1	⊗	1	3	2b 2a	⊗	3	2			X				X				X		7
✓ ♂ 904/56	1	2	1	⊗	⊗	3b 2b	⊗	2	3				X			X					X	6
♂ 905/57	3	3	1	3	⊗	3a 2b	⊗	3	3			X				X					X	7
♀ 906/58	1	2	1	⊗	⊗	⊗	⊗	3	3												X	5
♀ 907/59	2	3	3	⊗	⊗	3b 2b	⊗	3	3				X		X						X	6
♀ 908/60	3	3	3	3	⊗	3b 2b	⊗	3	3				X		X						X	7
♂ 909/61	3	3	3	3	⊗	2b 3b	⊗	3	3				X				X				X	7
	10	10	9	7	1	3		10	10													
♀ 100/42	3	2	3	3	⊗	3b 2a	⊗	2	3			X	/			X					X	7
♂ 101/62	2	2	3	⊗	3	3b 2a	⊗	2	3				X			X					X	7
♀ 102/63	3	3	3	3	⊗	3b 2a	⊗	3	3				X			X					X	7
♀ 103/64	3	3	3	3	⊗	3b 3b	⊗	3	3				X				X				X	7
✓ ♀ 104/65	1	2	2	1	⊗	2a 2b	⊗	2	2		X				X					X		7
✓ ♀ 105/66	3	3	3	3	⊗	2b 3a	⊗	3	3				X			X					X	7
✓ ♀ 106/67	1	3	3	2	⊗	3a 2a	⊗	3	3			X			X						X	7
♂ 107/68	3	2	3	3	⊗	2a 2b	⊗	3	3		X				X						X	7
♂ 108/69	2	3	3	2	⊗	3b 2a	⊗	3	3				X			X					X	7
♂ 109/70	3	3	3	3	⊗	3b 3b	⊗	3	3				X				X				X	7
♀ 110/71	3	3	3	3	⊗	2b 2a	⊗	2	3		X				X						X	7
	11	11	11	10	1	10		11	11													

(1) Comprehension of a class: the number of common qualities which are used in order to build up a set.

(2) Conservation: refers to the constitution of logical invariances.

(3) Conservation of number: the ability of the child to maintain constant a number of objects independently of its spatial disposition.

(4) Extension of a class: the numbers of individuals within a given class.

(5) Euclidean relationship: geometrical figures in accordance with principles of Euclid such as a triangle, rectangle, etc.

(6) Identity: a logical argument spontaneously used by the child to justify his belief in conservation implying that the transformation did not change the logical invariance.

(7) Logical equivalence: the ability of the child to maintain constant a number when the objects are placed in direct optical correspondence.

(8) Operatory behavior: behavior dealing with the mastery of simple concrete abstractions. The terms which follow dealing with more substantial definitions are borrowed from the newly published book of H. Furth.

(9) One-to-one correspondence: the ability to maintain in a one-to-one correspondence the same numbers of objects independently of their spatial organization.

(10) Perspectives: to spatial relationships and the ability of the child to change his point of view according to different observers.

(10a) Quantification of the extension: the ability to understand the generality of a logical classification without perceptual direct references.

(11) Reversibility: a logical argument spontaneously used by the child to justify his belief in conservation. This argument refers to the fact that one can come back to the point of departure.

(12) Seriation: logical relation dealing with the conservation of a certain constant order within the objects such as an increasing length, etc.

(13) Transitional: refers to a moment of the development where the child is at level 2, that is to say a level intermediary between level 1 and 3, where logic and perception get alternatively the upper hand.

(14) Subtraction of class: the ability to make logical subtractions.

(15) Topological relations: geometrical figures where global relations exist without being affected by changes in size or shapes. Relations of inside/outside and so on.

Action. A functional exchange between a biological organization and the environment that presupposes an internal structure and leads to a structuring of the environment. For Piaget, action if not limited to external action. It is generally synonymous with behavior.

Adaptation. A balanced state of biological organization within its environment. In behavior, an equilibration between assimilation and accommodation.

Assimilation. The incorporating process of an operative action. A taking in of environmental data, not in a casual, mechanistic sense, but as a function of an internal structure that by its own nature seeks activity through assimilation of potential material from the environment.

Concept. In a logical sense, a mental construct of the generalizable aspect of a known thing; it has an intension (or comprehension) answering the question. "What is its essence?" and an extension answering the question as to which things are exemplars of the concept. In a psychological sense, a concept is identical with an individual's internal structure of scheme and corresponds to the level of that structure (e.g. "Practical" concept). In its verbal manifestations, concept is a verbalized expression of a logical concept together with its verbalized comprehension; however, verbalization is extrinsic to the logical concept as such.

Concrete Operation. Characteristic of the first stage of operational intelligence. A concrete operation implies underlying general systems or "groupings" such as classification, seriation, number. Its applicability if limited to objects considered as real (concrete).

Conservation. The maintenance of a structure as invariant during physical changes of some aspects. The stability of an objective attribute is never simply given; it is constructed by the living organization. Conservation therefore implies an internal system of regulations that can compensate internally for external changes.

Coordination. The functional adaptation or the unifying form of the elements of an action, particularly of an external action though not limited to it; implies an active internal structure.

Equilibration. The internal regulatory factor underlying a biological organization; it is manifested in all life, particularly in the development and activity of intelligence. Intelligence makes explicit the regulations inherent in an organization. As a process, it is the regulatory factor that unifies evolution and development; as a state (an equilibrium), it is a continuously changing balancing of active compensations.

Formal Operation. Typically manifested in propositional thinking and a combinatory system that considers the real as one among other hypothetical possibilities. Formal operations are characteristic of the second and final stage of operational intelligence which "reflects" on concrete operations through the elaboration of formal "group" structures.

Language. The natural spoken (and heard) symbol system of communication typical of a society. One of the manifestations of symbol functioning. Language is acquired and used like other symbol behavior and chiefly influences intelligence indirectly through the social, educative impact of society.

Learning. In the strict sense, acquisition of knowledge due to some particular information provided by the environment. Learning is inconceivable with a theoretically prior interior structure of equilibration which provides the capacity to learn and the structuring of the learning process; in the wide sense, it includes both factors.

Logic. As a formalized system, can be employed to describe the structuring spontaneously manifest in intelligent behavior. The internal consistency and necessity of logical judgments command our intellectual assent. There is a continuous genetic relation between mature logical forms and prelogical structures of early behavior.

Operation. In the strict sense, the characteristic interiorized generalizable action of mature intelligence; an operation implies a structure through which: (1) the resulting "knowing" need not be exteriorized as in sensorimotor intelligence, and (2) an operation is reversible, it can turn in an inverse direction and thus negate its own activity. In the wide sense, operational is here taken to include preoperational but exclude sensorimotor actions.

Operativity. Contrasted with figurative knowledge it implies the action aspect of intelligence at all periods, including sensorimotor intelligence. Operativity is the essential, generalizable structuring aspect of intelligence insofar as knowing means constructing, transforming, incorporating, etc.

Organization. The most general expression of the form of a biological organism, a totality in which elements are related to each other and to the whole, the totality itself being related to a greater totality. The functioning of the organism gives content to the organization. All biological phenomena including intelligence and evolution find their basic explanation in the biological organization. An organization has intrinsic regulatory mechanisms.

Pre-operational. Often used to designate the period after the sensorimotor stage but prior to the formation of the first operations in the strict sense. The pre-operational period is the preparatory part of the stage of concrete operational intelligence, characterized by the deforming need for symbolic support, hence egocentrism.

Reversibility. The possibility of performing a given action in a reversed direction. Its two chief forms are negation (not male-female) and reciprocity (not better-worse). Reversibilty is the criterion of an underlying operational structure.

Stages. Successive developmental periods of intelligence, each one characterized by a relatively stable general structure that incorporates developmentally earlier structures in a higher synthesis. The regular sequence of stage-specific activities is decisive for intellectual development rather than chronological age.

Structure. The general form, the interrelatedness of parts within an organized totality. Structure can often be used interchangeably with organization, system, form, coordination.

Transformation. As external transformation, refers to the constantly changing appearance of the physical world. As internal transformation, refers to knowing as constructing invariants through which external changes can be internally compensated for. Operations are internal transformations relative to an invariant and consequently they lead to an objective understanding of physical changes.

References

1. A. Binet. Etude experimentale de l'intelligence.
2. D. Wechsler. The measurement of adult intelligence, 3 ed. Williams and Wilkins, Baltimore (1944).
3. D.E. Berlyne. Structure and direction in thinking. Wiley, New York (1965).
4. D. Krech et al. Individual in society. McGraw-Hill, New York (1962).
5. J. Bruner. Studies in cognitive growth. Wiley, New York (1966).
6. M. Bovet. Etudes interculturelles du développement intellectuel et processus d'apprentissage. Revue Suisse de Psychologie Vol. 27 (1968).
7. D.M. Hyde. An investigation of Piaget's theories of the development of the concept of number. Unpublished Doctoral Dissertation, University of London (1959).
8. B.W. Estes. Some mathematical and logical concepts in children. J. Genet. Psychol. 88 (1956).
9. E. Feigenbaum and J. Feldman. Computers and thought. McGraw-Hill, New York (1963).
10. S. Papert and G. Voyat. A propos du perception, in: Etudes d'épistémologie génétique, Vol. XXII. Presses Universitaires de France (1968).
11. P. Radin. Primitive man as a philosopher. Dover, New York (1959).
12. E. Cassirer. Das Erkenntnisproblem, Vol. 1, Berlin (1906).
13. Lévy-Brühl. La mentalité primitive. Alcan, Paris (1922).
14. J. Piaget. Introduction à l'épistémologie génétique, Vol. II. Presses Universitaires de France (1950).
15. N. Chomsky. Syntactic structures. Mouton, The Hague (1964).
16. E. Maynard and G. Twiss. That these people may live. Community Mental Health Program (1969).
17. E. Erikson. Childhood and society, 2 ed. Norton, New York (1963).
18,19. M. Wax et al. Formal education in an Indian American community. SSSP Monograph, Vol. 11, No. 4 (1964).
20. J. Piaget. The moral judgment in the child. Kegan Paul, London (1932).

156

21. L. Kohlberg. Development of moral judgment and of the sense of justice in the years 10 to 16. Paper read at APA meeting, Washington, DC (1958).

22. S. Papert and G. Voyat. Le temps et l'épistémologie génétique, in: Perception et notion du temps. Etudes d'épistémologie génétique, Vol. XXI. Presses Universitaires de France (1968).

23. J.S. Bruner. Inhelder and Piaget's "The growth of logical thinking, I," A psychologist's point of view. Brit. J. Psychol. 50 (1959).

24. J. Piaget. On the development of memory and identity. Heinz Werner Lecture Series, Vol. II (1968).

25. J. Piaget. Six psychological studies. Vintage Books, New York (1967).

26. H. Furth. Thinking without language. Free Press, New York (1966).

27. B. Inhelder and J. Piaget. The early growth of logic in the child, Norton, New York (1964).

28. H. Sinclair de Zwart. Developmental psycholinguistics, in: Studies in cognitive development. Oxford University Press, New York (1969).

29. B. Inhelder. Le diagnostic du raisonnement chez les débiles mentaux. Delachaux et Nestlé, Neuchâtel (1944).

30. J. Wohlwill and R.C. Lowe. An experimental analysis of the development of the conservation of number. Child Development 33 (1962).

31. J. Bruner. The process of education. Harvard University Press, Cambridge (1961).

32. J. Smedslund. The acquisition of the conservation of substance and weight. Scand. J. Psych. 2 (1961).

32a. E.A. Pell. An experimental examination of some of Piaget's schemata concerning children's perception and thinking. Brit. J. Educ. Psychol. 29 (1959).

32b. E.A. Hunzer. Recent studies in Britain based on the work of J. Piaget. Nat. Found. Educ. Res. Wales, England (London) (1960).

32c. J. Wohlwill. A study of the development of the number concept by scalogram analysis. J. Genet. Psychol. 97 (1960).

33,34. J. Piaget. The child's conception of number. Humanities, New York (1952).

35. J. Piaget. The child's conception of geometry. Basic Books, New York (1960).

36. J. Flavell. The developmental psychology of J. Piaget. Van Nostrand, New York (1963).

37. J. Mehler and T. Bever. Cognitive capacity of very young children. Science 158:3797 (1967).

38. J. Piaget and B. Inhelder. The child's conception of space. Routledge and Kegan Paul, London (1956).

39. W.E. Vinacke. The psychology of thinking. McGraw-Hill, New York (1952).

40. V. Hazlitt. Children's thinking. Brit. J. Psychol. 20 (1930).
41. M. Annett. The classification of four common class concepts
     by children and adults. Brit. J. Psychol. 29 (1959).
42. B. Inhelder et al. Développement et apprentissage. Revue
     Suisse de Psychologie Vol. 26, No. 1 (1967).
43. J. Piaget. Psychologie et pédagogie. Denoel, Paris (1969).
44. C. Kami. Preparing pre-school children for the acquisition of
     elementary number concepts. Proceedings of the Conference
     of New England Kindergarten Teachers, Boston (1969).
45. C. Kami and N. Radin. A framework for pre-school curriculum
     based on Piaget's theory, in: Educational implications
     of Piaget's theory. Atney and Rudabeau (1969).
46. C. Kami et al. A Piaget derived pre-school curriculum. Young
     Children 2 (1967).
47. A. Jensen. How much can one boost scholastic achievement?
     Harvard Educational Review, Spring (1969).
48. P. Henninger and H. Eposito. Indian schools. Review of Books,
     New York (1969).
49. G. Voyat. IQ--God made or man-made? Saturday Review, May
     (1969).
50. J. Piaget. The genetic approach to the psychology of thought.
51. Vine Deloria, Jr. Custer died for your sins. Macmillan, New York
     (1969).
52. F.J. Bryde. Modern Indian psychology. Bryde and BIA (1967).
53. A. Schorr. Poor kids. Basic Books, New York (1966).
54. K. Mindell. Statement to Senate Subcommittee on Indian
     Education, April (1968).
55. R.M. Utley. The last days of the Sioux nation. Yale
     University Press, New Haven (1963).

Index